THE
NUTS AND BOLTS
OF ERECTING A CONTRACTING EMPIRE

YOUR **COMPLETE GUIDE** FOR
BUILDING **SUCCESS** IN THE
CONSTRUCTION, **CONTRACTING**,
AND **TRADESMAN** INDUSTRIES

JOEL ANDERSON

The Nuts and Bolts of Erecting a Contracting Empire

Your Complete Guide for Building Success in the Construction, Contracting, and Tradesman Industries

Joel Anderson

Published by Nuts and Bolts Contracting, LLC

www.NutsandBoltsContracting.com

ISBN: 978-0692126714

I/A # 19051801INT

Foreword

Achieving success in a business endeavor may seem to be the result of mysterious and sometimes loosely defined processes. Those accomplishing it are often regarded with reverence, their business acumen considered more a magical "knack" they have rather than the application of any exact technology.

There is ample information covering various parts of running a business, but there is little out there that shows how to put it all together to create a thriving business. The construction industry is no exception. This vital industry is full of folks with great competence in their own trades, many of whom have learned the important mechanics of management such as CPM (Critical Path Method of scheduling), accounting, material take-off, etc., yet many remain, by their own estimation, clueless on to how to achieve an overall thriving construction enterprise.

Luckily, it turns out that achieving a prosperous business, in construction or otherwise, is not dependent on finding that elusive "success dust." Success is achieved by knowing and applying good basic organizational technology.

There are actual steps that can be taken that nearly guarantee success. There are essentials that are easy to learn and understand, and most importantly, to apply. These essentials become the bedrock to a business that operates smoothly and with certainty. The days of coping with minor and major disasters, feast and famine, of barely holding it together will be a thing of the past.

Joel Anderson and I have been professional colleagues and friends for nearly twenty years. We have worked on scores of projects together. Whenever Joel is involved, projects simply move along smoothly.

I recall a time nearly a decade ago in a particularly interesting circumstance when I had been asked to provide engineering for a facility that would be used by the public. It was composed of intricate structures including stages, a skating rink, several displays, and small buildings. This project had to be permitted, engineered, approved, inspected, and built to code and, very uniquely, was temporary and would be taken down in about two months.

And it was to be executed by volunteers with hardly any experience in construction.

Due to the nearly impossible situation, Joel was called in, due to his apparent "magic," to pull this off to a successful conclusion. I saw him organize this group of inexperienced, though eager, volunteers into a successful construction team. Within a short time the project was done—on schedule and within budget. It successfully opened to thousands of delighted youngsters and families. Joel did this on the side and as a volunteer.

Many have discovered Joel's unique abilities in organizing people and operations, especially in construction. He has become the go-to guy for many institutions and individuals who need someone to come in to make things go right in their construction company, projects, and challenges.

And, of course, he has grown his own contracting business into a grand success (steel fabrication and construction), orchestrating large building projects throughout the country.

Aside from Joel's operational talents and reputation, his credentials are no less impressive. He is a licensed state-certified general contractor, served journeyman as an electrician, plumber, pipe fitter, carpenter, steel fabricator, HVAC expert, mechanic, welder, and more. He has won numerous awards in various areas including contractor safety and trade logistics. He was honorary chairman of the President's National Business Advisory Council; he was a steel construction pricing consultant for the US Department of Labor and he was listed on the Strathmore's Who's Who in Building

Engineering. He has also been recognized for other outstanding achievements in the construction or tradesman industry.

The tools Joel introduces in this book were not acquired when he earned his Business Arts degree. These tools and methods were learned afterwards, through decades of hard-won experience. He developed them through his own actions as well as studying and applying key organizational philosophies, the fundamental concepts of organization.

This book is an outline of the basics of organizing and running any construction-oriented enterprise. He addresses key concepts that remain mostly untouched in other studies of organizational resources including finance, production, quality control, obtaining new business, and the basics of operation.

He emphasizes key concepts and definitions that are usually brushed off as being "already known by everyone," yet are not. These basic concepts are usually misunderstood or not even considered by most people, even by mentors and teachers in the subject.

And he makes it all clear and easy to understand.

I've noticed that successful people seem to make what they do look easy. I believe this is because they have mastered certain key and basic concepts of their own crafts. If a subject appears complicated, it is a clue that that it is not well understood. As Albert Einstein said, "If you can't explain it to a six-year-old, you don't understand it yourself." We're not six-year-olds, but the power of mastered simple concepts is still the real key to competence and understanding.

Joel introduces and clarifies basic concepts and provides checklists and worksheets for application. The reader of this book won't just learn, but will be given tools he or she can use to apply these principles.

I am happy to know Joel and to introduce you to this book. And I eagerly welcome you to a new realm of success in your own endeavors.

Ken Risley, Professional Engineer and Certified General Contractor

Table of Contents

Dedication

There are many who deserve mention here. Unfortunately, naming all of them would create a book much larger than this one.

First and foremost, I dedicate this book to my wife, Pam, who is my best friend and partner in life. Through the years she has endured, shared, and supported me in my failures and successes. Fortunately, successes are much more common for us now!

To my family, all of whom saw great potential in me and supported me in my endeavors.

To all the masters in their crafts whom I have had the pleasure to apprentice under. You have given me knowledge and wisdom found in no books.

To all my associates whom I have had the great satisfaction of working with.

To all my friends on my journey through life as well as those I have yet to meet.

Without the inspiration from these people and the life experiences we shared, I would have probably never chosen such a path of happiness and accomplishment.

Introduction

Many people start their own business without realizing what is involved in running a company. Good people, people with the best intentions at heart and goals in mind. People who genuinely want to help others achieve their goals by providing them with a valuable product and/or service.

Then the nightmares begin. Perhaps you're very good at your trade but have little or no idea how to correctly form a company, run a business, keep up with the laws or regulations, and bring in new customers—let alone keep track of projects, employees, and accounting practices.

You find yourself having to learn how to do so many things that it becomes over-whelming, even crushing at times. Even if you try to seek out help, the answers you get to the problems you are facing are not always right, causing more heartache. These things prevent you from having the time or energy to perform your craft, which actually makes the income. Money becomes difficult to generate. You feel like a rat in a maze that has no exit!

The reason I wrote this book is to help provide answers by utilizing simple yet proven solutions to the problems you face when operating a company, small or large.

In my forty-six years in the construction and contracting business I have faced every one of the problems you encounter and some you haven't yet. I have spent almost half a century finding the answers that have helped me on the path to success, building and selling three companies as well as rescuing dying entities from the ashes of failure. My goal is to help you avoid the mistakes I (and so many other entrepreneurs) made early on and achieve your goals and dreams.

My answers are definitely not the only ones out there. There are as many systems for running a business as there are people dreaming them up. They all resemble each other in one way or another. What works for one may not work for another.

My goal in creating this book was to develop a set of principles and practices to help any construction or contracting (or tradesman or mechanic) enterprise avoid mistakes and navigate through or around that maze. These are principles and practices that, when followed, allow you to establish and continually improve the basis of operations all the way up the line.

That is what is contained within these pages. It is a master's degree from the School of Hard Knocks. It is a doctorate degree from the Graduate University of Trial and Error. It is the culmination of trying damn near every system available and only keeping the elements of each that proved to be usable and beneficial.

I wrote this book in simple, easy-to-understand language and stayed away from all the big words and complex terms, primarily because all those do is confuse the hell out of me and they really play no role in teaching. If there is a word or term that you don't understand in this book, you'll find it in any common dictionary.

I wish you the greatest success in the pursuit of your dreams and the achievement of your success as you erect your contracting empire.

How to Use This Book

I f your company is involved in any type of contracting, construction, or tradesman endeavor, you will find this book is packed with information that will help you organize your business and take it to the next level.

At the end of each chapter you will see a basic exercise for organizing your company on a flow chart. Performing these exercises will help your company become more organized and operate at a higher level of efficiency.

In reading the chapters of this book, there will be sentences marked by a number at the end. These numbers correspond with the last page of the chapter where each number identifies the source reference and gives additional information as well as supporting quotes by other accomplished authors or entrepreneurs.

Many of the concepts, principles and practices contained within this book are through my education and successful application of the Hubbard® Management System (HMS), which is based on the works of L. Ron Hubbard. As mentioned, I have put many administrative systems to the acid test during my career and the HMS is the one system that works all the time when understood and used.

The 12 volume *Hubbard College of Administration Reference* set lays out the exact theory and application of the HMS — you can obtain this set through the website hubbardcollegepress.org.

The sample flow chart page is there to show you a basic format of organization. Although the size is impractical to use in the real world, we offer you two choices to get one you can use: digital or hard copy via snail mail—both are free. Simply go to http://www.NutsandBoltsContracting.com/chart to get your copy.

To gain the full benefit of this book and apply all the key concepts, I highly recommend *The Nuts and Bolts Companion Workbook*. The workbook, as you fill it out, becomes the owner's manual for your company. It is available on Amazon and at www.NutsandBoltsContracting.com.

I wish you great success.

Joel Anderson

Chapter One

THE BASICS OF OWNERSHIP

Almost every business owner I have had the pleasure of meeting has moved from employee to business owner to fulfill his or her goals and dreams.

Reasons for this are varied but they go something like this: "I could do way better work if the boss didn't stand in my way" or "Starting my own company will make it so I can make more money" or "I can be even more successful than my boss because he doesn't do things like he should" and even "My boss has no idea of what he's doing; I know I could do way better." Chances are these reasons are 100 percent correct. What I am saying here is that *you are right*.

You see, your boss most likely started his business for the same reasons you did, and he too did not realize what was involved in establishing, operating, and expanding a company.

Whatever reasons you have had to own a business, it was at the very least to pursue your goals and dreams—to make your journey through life better!

There is another classic reason you ended up owning a company—you took over the family business. Usually that situation goes one of two ways: "Dad was always a welder and he had his own metal fabrication shop so it's only right that I carry on with what he taught me" or "Dad made me work in the family business since I could walk and I don't want any part of it, but somehow I got stuck with it anyway."

A company or business is the type of vehicle that propels one down the road of life and it does not come with an owner's manual. When you buy a new car, truck, or piece of equipment, you're excited. You watch all the instructional videos, watch YouTube videos on how other people use that model, and browse the owner's manual to find out things you never knew about its features. You look in every nook and cranny of it, see how it operates in different conditions, and run it hard. If you have a problem with it, what do you do first? Where do you look? In the manual. It takes care of you and you it. You *own* it. And by that I mean you *make it your own!*

As a tradesman you own your craft. You are an expert, do beautiful work, you're at the top of your game. No one can touch your performance. But as the owner of your own company you are constantly being pulled into the business side of things. This takes time away from performing the work you so love. It is a forever aggravation and sucks all your spare time dry. It causes problems in other areas of life and problems for your company and the business activities it is involved in. Your family or friends get mad because you're never free. You have no time for social activities that you enjoy. Having been there myself, I know your pain.

As a business owner you have undoubtedly realized that there is way more to it than you first realized and you still have a *lot* to learn. You have searched for answers on the internet; you've called your friends, parents, or associates for help.

This is where it gets interesting, right? The answers you get are all different! When every answer seems to lead to more confusion, how do you decide what answer to pick? This isn't your fault, but it is your responsibility. A tough break for sure, and some days you end up kicking yourself in the ass. Enough of this time after time and you think, "Geeze, maybe my boss was not so bad after all; I had no idea he was going through all this crap."

You one day came up with a tickling in your brain that you had to find a way that works. There must be tools to use or a plan to follow—a blueprint for business somewhere that you can use to guarantee your success and the success of your company. You had to find that owner's manual that teaches you how to run your company and get your life back. After all, other people do have successful businesses, why not you, right?

Everyone who has a successful business, whether it be a sales or service company, takes complete responsibility for it. He or she has **ownership.** That person is the owner, knows he or she is the owner, has made the decision to be the source of the company's existence as well as take full charge for all the ups and downs it goes through and all the work involved in making it expand to new levels. They also have a structured format they follow which, over time, through trial and error, has become the owner's manual for their company.

Well, I do have good news—an owner's manual can exist for your business. And here is the real shocker—*you* are going to write it! That's right, you are going to write it. Just like different models of cars, different businesses need different manuals.

I can hear you saying, "What?!?! *Me* write it"? Yes, you write it. Using the simple organizing tools, economic basics, and proven methods of administration that are behind every successful business. It is not as tough as you might think. You'll find all the proven principles and practices laid out in the chapters in this book.

Whether you are a one-person show, have 5 employees, or have 500, these stable tools, principles, and practices apply to your company.

You see, you already know where you have the most difficulty: "those business things." But "those business things" can be understood and applied by you. I assure you, I am being 100 percent honest with you.

Before we get started on your manual, we have a lot more to cover in this chapter about your ownership position in your company. Being the owner of your business puts you at the top of the ladder. From that top rung, you are in the position to see what is occurring on the landscape of the organization around you. You have to know what's happening. You are, or will be, the top executive in your company. The advantage you have is that you started at the bottom rung, in one way or another.

Below are the key points you will be addressing in taking full ownership of your company and the managing of it:

1. **BUSINESS STRUCTURE:** Organizing the establishment of your company. How you arrange and assemble the component parts of your company to operate like a fine Swiss watch. This can be done with a very simple organization chart which shows who does what in different parts of the company in order to end up producing and selling the company's products and services. Have you ever walked into a shop and watched the employees and wondered how they get anything done? Half of them are looking at their cell phones and the other half don't know what their function is let alone what they are supposed to be doing. Or the shop where everyone is working like mad but it takes you a month to get a simple thing made. You keep calling to find out why you don't have your thing yet, and you just keep being bounced around to different people on the phone, getting no answers. There is no organizational structure here to follow.

2. **COMPANY IMAGE:** What do you want current and future customers to see? This first impression is very important. If you had a guy show up for an appointment to give you an estimate on a job in an old broken-down truck who looked like he just crawled out of a mud hole, what would you think? You would think you don't want anything to do with him. Or how many times have you walked into a supply house and the place is an utter war zone? Not only can't you wait to get out of there, you wonder if the part you bought is even the right one!

3. **COMPANY FACILITIES:** Do you rent? Do you want your own building? More importantly how are those facilities maintained and repaired, and who does it? I am talking about your offices, shop, trucks, tools, equipment, and anything else that is crucial in performing your work.

It's pretty embarrassing when the truck breaks down all the time or the generator won't run when you get to the job site. Those things cost time, money, and really piss people off, both employees because they cannot efficiently do the job and customers because you're not doing your job.

4. **COMPANY POLICY:** Do you have your own company policy? This is the dos and don'ts for all company employees, no matter what their seniority is, to follow in a manner which promotes unity for the organization in its endeavors. Remember, it does include you, too. As the owner, everyone in the company will follow what you do. You lead by example. If you do not follow your own company policy, they won't either and you end up with each employee going their own way. What I mean here is: doing what they think they should, based on what they have done in some previous business or were taught somewhere else. You don't want that to occur because it divides the organization and takes morale into the toilet. This exact thing is where you see companies that have little cliques in every department, each one doing their own thing, usually having very little to do with what the company as a whole is doing. But if you're not a part of the clique and do what you know you should do, then you are a snitch or whatever it's called these days. We've all been there. I have even had to stamp that fire out in my own companies.

5. **LEGALITIES:** Are your licenses current and correct for the scope of work you perform? Do you have adequate and current insurances: worker's comp; general liability; vehicle and equipment? Are all your posters in place for employees to see as required by law? Do you have a current set of code or compliance regulations for your activities to refer to? Do you have current OSHA standards for your industry and do you enforce following them while performing your services? I see more companies with legal compliance issues than I care to count. Yet, these are very important in protecting the company from fines, lawsuits, attacks, and so forth. Whether or not you have these things in place makes a direct impact on who will use your company. Having all these ducks in a row will give you more leverage when going after the bigger jobs that help expand your company and its reputation.

6. **INTERNAL MANAGEMENT COORDINATION:** Big words, I know. It simply means having the correct communications with the leaders of each section of the company so all the effort is shared shoulder to shoulder, pushing that wheel of progress along the road to success. Do you have weekly planning, production, or coordination meetings? You know, the sales division just closed a $100,000 contract and doesn't tell anybody so two weeks go by before the shop finds out and now you have to make up two weeks right out of the gate to get the job done on time. Geeze!!!

7. **THE FUTURE OF YOUR COMPANY:** What are your short- and long-term goals for your company? In a year what is the growth you would like to see? Five years? Do you have an exit strategy for when you have achieved these goals? In other words, selling your company for top dollar and moving into a higher level of life or even starting another company.

Now that you have reviewed the above seven key points having to do with ownership of your company, let's get you to work on a couple of basic exercises that help you begin to organize its structure. The point of these exercises is to help you develop an understanding of the importance of fully taking charge of your company and organizing it effectively. In the Companion Workbook, there are many more exercises to help you bring your company to a new level of success. You can just do very basic writing or create any fancy or elaborate book that you like. The point of these exercises is to develop an understanding, a path to follow that you can refer back to when things get confused.

As you go through this book and do the exercises you will discover things about yourself. You will become educated with information that will help you organize and run your company more efficiently. You will actually see, feel, and experience positive changes as you do these exercises and then start using what you have learned in your company and your life. This will then give you better control of your path in business and in life. You will see abilities you never knew you had, leading you to new ideas and better ways of solving problems.

At some point, you will go back and modify your owner's manual to better serve you, your employees, the products or services that you perform, and your company as a whole. In fact, as you and your company grow, you may end up modifying it several times to suit your needs. It has been said that the journey of a thousand miles begins with the first step. So let's get you walking on the path to success, both personally and professionally, right now!

EXERCISE: OWNERSHIP

Write down what it means to you to be the owner of your company. What are the things that you do or that you can do to have full ownership of your company? How do you take full responsibility for the whole operation? How do you know, without a doubt, that you are the owner? What actions do you take that firmly make you the source of the company's performance? Write down anything and everything you can think of with regards to your ownership of the company. When you really feel like you are the owner of your company and you can perform the actions of the owner no matter how difficult or uncomfortable, then you have achieved the mindset of a business owner and you are done with this exercise.

Now here is a little note: ownership also includes an executive or manager in a top leadership role for a company. No matter what size the company is, if you lead a section or sections of the company, ownership applies to you. You may not *own* it, *per se*, but if you don't have ownership for it, you will not reach your full potential in guiding your section towards success. So this book and these exercises are for you too!

EXERCISE: BUSINESS STRUCTURE

On the next page is a basic chart of the fundamental components of a company structure which show its individual operations. (Note: you can download a full-size version of this chart either as an electronic file or request a hard copy which will be sent to you via snail mail at www.NutsandBoltsContracting.com/chart.) You'll notice that there are many positions below owner. And as you know, you hold most or all of those positions at some time or another during the course of your operating your company.

First, look at all the headings. Read and get to know each section. You will get to understand all the things you and/or your employees do to keep your company running. How well you list these things out in the correct section will determine how well each corresponding area of your company gets managed.

You will find that there are more hats you wear than you originally thought. This is likely to get to a "holy crap" moment when you realize how much you really do and do right.

We are going to keep this exercise simple. For now, just list all the key points one through seven of ownership in this chapter in the first column under the heading "Executive Manager" on the chart, leaving some space in between each item. Then under each key point list out all the things you do with, concerning, or about that point as the owner of your company.

You can do this on the page or duplicate the page into a nice big chart you put on the wall in your office for all to see. Now pay attention here. Because when others can see this chart showing them everything it takes to keep your company running, you can then assign an employee or employees to that section to perform those functions. You have just lightened your workload!

I have seen these charts eight feet high and twenty feet long in companies with hundreds of people on a wall in plain sight where every employee can see it. It makes everyone feel part of something. They take pride in knowing they are a part of something real, how it all works, and what work they need to do to get to the top.

You will come back to this chart and fill in the remaining sections with what you learn as you progress through each of the remaining chapters in this book.

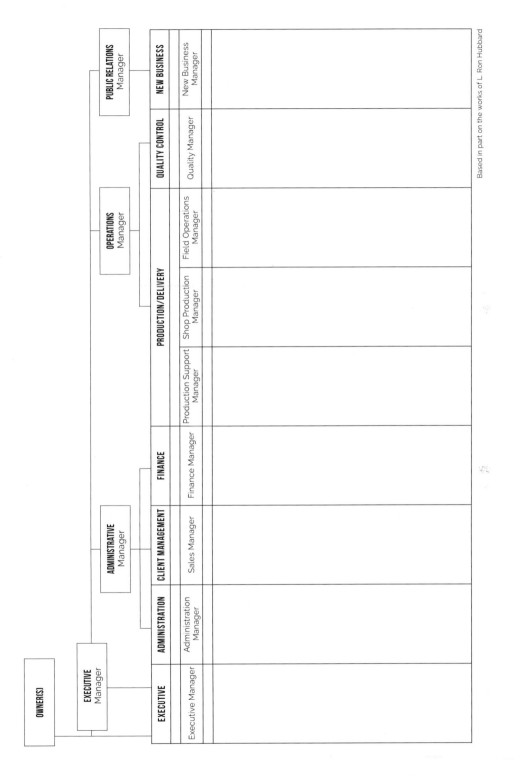

OWNER(S)

EXECUTIVE Manager

ADMINISTRATIVE Manager

OPERATIONS Manager

PUBLIC RELATIONS Manager

EXECUTIVE	ADMINISTRATION	CLIENT MANAGEMENT	FINANCE	PRODUCTION/DELIVERY			QUALITY CONTROL	NEW BUSINESS
Executive Manager	Administration Manager	Sales Manager	Finance Manager	Production Support Manager	Shop Production Manager	Field Operations Manager	Quality Manager	New Business Manager

Based in part on the works of L. Ron Hubbard

SUMMARY

Congratulations on completing Chapter One and getting going on being the owner of your company. You are starting to write the owner's manual for your company. What you have done so far and what you will be doing is helping you organize your company into a well-oiled machine.

There are a few things you will notice occurring as you continue to do this. You will notice employees change. Most will change for the better and a few will fight what you're doing. Keep an eye on those fighting you; if they don't come around and get with the team, you'll have to let them go.

You will notice a team spirit amongst the employees. They will feel a sense of worth. They will begin to go above and beyond because they will be working for the same purpose and not just as individuals.

You may face sections of the company blowing up at times because as you organize, all the disorganization that has been present can explode like a bomb. Don't worry, when the dust settles, keep on organizing and streamlining operations.

I would be at fault if I didn't close with this little tidbit. As an owner, or an executive in a leadership role, there are some precautions you must take in governing your people. We will cover these precautions in the following chapters. You will see and understand as you continue reading how and why people accept good management and rebel against bad management.

Here is the main thing to watch—because you are organizing the operations and direction of your company in a totally aligned purpose you will see it grow from **your** company into **the** company. Employees will take responsibility for their areas like never before. Your workload will lessen until you are the maestro standing up in front, conducting the orchestra.

THE DIFFERENCE BETWEEN	
BOSS	**LEADER**
Drives Employees	Guides Employees
Places Blame for a Problem	Helps Fix the Problem
Depends on Seniority	Recognizes Equality
Abuses People	Honors People
Always says "I"	Always says "We"
Only Takes Credit	Always Gives Credit
Demands "NOW!"	Requests "When?"
Threatens Character	Strengthens Integrity
Screams and Belittles	Explains and Encourages
Says "Damn Good Thing"	Says "Thank You"

As my grandfather used to say, "You get more flies with honey than you do shit."

Chapter Two

THE BASICS OF ADMINISTRATION

Before we dive into this section of the company, let's have a look at what *administration* is—what the word means. It simply means, "the management of any office, company or organization" according to the dictionary.[*]

The first part of a company's administration simply manages the hiring, training, and morale of employees. The next part handles the communications in to, around, and out of the company. The final part of this section monitors the organization, including its employees and operations, so that all the sections can work together to achieve a well-established company producing high-quality products and services.

It only makes sense to have a part of a company section devoted to the people who make the company. Without human resources helping employees through their

---

[*] http://www.dictionary.com/browse/administration?s=t

difficulties, you can't be very successful building a formidable team. Be absolutely sure that the employees are rewarded when they do good and give them help in the areas they struggle with.

How many times have you been in someone else's business and asked one of their employees for help? You didn't get the help you wanted but you sure heard an earful of what is wrong with the business. Well, nobody is being responsible for the employee's morale, checking with them to find out how they are doing and how well they like what they do for the company. This is all too common. The left hand doesn't even know it has a right hand. No communication occurs or bad communication dominates the workplace.

Do they know what their job is and how it fits in with what all the other employees are doing to create the final products and services of the company? How is their family doing? Are their kids OK? Do they feel that they are taken care of properly by you and the company?

Now don't misunderstand me here. I am not saying you let people walk all over you because you're a "nice guy" (or gal). You are their leader. I tell all my employees this: "Don't mistake my kindness for ignorance."

Or this happens: No one performs the employees' scheduled evaluations so they aren't acknowledged for their contributions to the company. Or worse yet, something they are doing wrong, or not doing that they should be, goes unnoticed and stays the hidden source of problems you can never find. If an employee feels that no one cares, or that there's no chance of moving up in the company, that is the point you will see your best employee become your worst nightmare.

Employee evaluations are important for two reasons: one, to rate employees' performance and service to the company and two, to give a cost-of-living pay increase as a result of an excellent report or let the employee know what he or she has to do, improve, or change in order to advance to the next rung on the ladder or level of pay at their next evaluation term.

And know this as well: if a person can't be or refuses to be helped no matter how hard you try, get rid of them. They will only make your business an impossible place to be for anyone, employees and customers alike. It is that simple. Do not keep them around.

The communications part of this section addresses the incoming mail and distributes it to the proper employee in the proper section. It makes sure all the incoming phone calls and any internet traffic get transferred to their respective areas and employees of the company. Everything going out of the company is taken care of as well—all the communications on whatever platforms are used are sent to and arrive at their intended destination.

And the issue that gets most overlooked in way too many businesses ... the communications between departments and employees in those departments. Finance doesn't tell client management that client X never paid their bill, so the bill never gets paid. Administration never tells the shop manager there is a new employee starting on Monday, so the person shows up in the shop first thing in the morning Monday and nobody is there to greet him and put him to work, so the person leaves. I could go on and on but you get the idea. It just doesn't work out too well when the organization doesn't communicate with itself.

Have you ever filled out a "request for more information" form on a website? I have. I have waited from weeks to months before I ever got an answer or have never gotten an answer at all. Of course, I didn't wait for the answer because when I didn't have it in a day or so I found another source for what I needed and bought it from them. Now, realize I am not the only one filling that form out. Think of all the business that company never does because there is no one in the company handling that communication line.

Here's another one that can really get to you: You call your supplier and order materials and they say the materials will be there in a week. So, a week later you go there to pick them up and they aren't ready. The counter guy can't even find a record showing that you placed an order. He finally finds it on the phone-order guy's desk, but your materials were never ordered from the warehouse. After an hour or so you are ready to rip someone's eyes out. Your job is delayed, your customer is livid, and now the field crew has no work to do. Damn it, man!

You already know that the fastest way to anger a customer is to not deliver their order in the agreed-upon time. When you see a company that has very few or no repeat customers you can be damn sure they operate that way. They almost always deliver their products or their contract completion dates on services way too late. The rocket science behind this is that the company has lousy or no communication channels internally or with its customers.

By being involved in what actually occurs on any given day and monitoring what goes on in the business you can be a security force for the company. You can find problem areas in the company through precise monitoring then develop and implement the necessary steps to correct that area.

OK. So how does one do this? Very easily actually. The first way is by observation and talking to the employees. Every morning after things get rolling take a walk around the company, look at what is happening, say good morning to people, and ask them how it's going.

Is the place hustling along, everybody working together? If not, look at what's happening and find the problem. If you can't readily spot it, ask your employees what is going on; this can give you an idea of where to look. But this is just the first step; don't ever take someone's word for what the problem is—look and find it for yourself. Remember, a leader helps fix the problem.

Here's why. Let's say you notice that the widget machine isn't making widgets as fast as it should be. You ask the operator what the problem is, and he tells you, "the machine has been acting funny ever since the power went out last week." If you listened to this then you would believe that some control was blown up, something that required a factory tech to come out and find and fix the problem at some huge expense.

And to make sure no further damage occurred you would shut the machine down until the tech could get there. Now no widgets would be produced, and you have presold orders that have delivery dates coming up. This would end up in disaster for sure.

Instead you look at the machine. Everything seems fine, it is making perfect widgets, it's just running too slow. You look at the control panel, check for the proper position of all the individual switches, and find that there is a switch in the wrong position. When the operator started the batch of widgets he put the machine in "Set-up" mode, like he should have. When he verified the widgets were coming out to specifications, he should have moved the switch to the "Run" mode and he didn't.

You point to the switch and have him look at it. After a look of horror, he flips the switch to "Run" and the machine runs perfectly at the right speed.

Now, you can see what would have happened had you taken his word and not looked for yourself. But you don't stop there. You find out why he didn't flip the switch and take care of that problem too so that kind of thing doesn't keep reoccurring.

As you walk through the organization you are going to find things you won't believe have been occurring—both minor things and chances are a few big ones. At first you're going to wonder how anything progressed in a positive way. Don't get discouraged though, the more you do this the less and less you will find wrong.

* * *

The second way you monitor the company is by statistical information. Ah, there's some more big words. What is a statistic? It is simply a fact or a graph that shows the value of something. It shows what is happening in a visual way, so the information can be used to find out what is happening in any activity. Have a look at this sample graph.

The sample graph is VERY easy to read. You don't really even need values on it. You can see that something drove that line up 3 days in a row. On day 5 something changed and it went down like diving off a cliff. On day 6 it didn't go up or down.

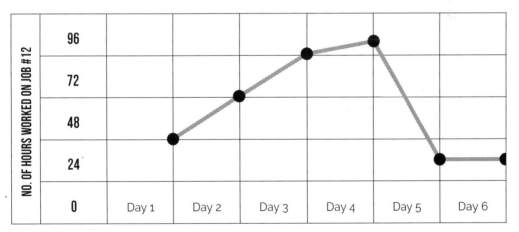

OK. Now, what would you do with this information? You'd find out what made the line go up and keep doing whatever that was. You'd find out what made the line dive off and you find a problem to correct and correct it.[1] Just what made those things happen?

Here is an example to fit that graph: You have a six-man crew doing framing on a house. You do some recon and find out that the wall material showed up on day one, on days two, three, and four the whole crew showed up and worked very well, completing all the exterior walls.

The roof trusses were supposed to arrive on day four, but the truss company didn't deliver the trusses to the jobsite. And no one from the truss company called and on day five you can't reach them either. Your crew did their job perfectly so the trusses could go in on day five. You find out that since the trusses never showed up on day four, then on days five and six, only two guys showed up for work and didn't even put in a full day. There are several things wrong here:

- **THE TRUSS COMPANY'S SCREW UP ON DELIVERY**
- **NO COMMUNICATION FROM THE JOBSITE**
- **NO COMMUNICATION FROM THE TRUSS COMPANY**
- **ONLY TWO GUYS SHOWING UP FOR WORK ON DAYS FIVE AND SIX**

You can realize two basic truths here. There is no ownership in the truss company and there is no ownership for your jobsite. No one is leading either of these. You may not be able to fix the truss company problem, but you can sure switch to dealing with a more reputable company.

As far as your jobsite foreman goes, you can fix that problem with simple instruction. You coach him and get him to understand how these types of things can be prevented, even if just by calling the office at noon and saying, "Hey, it's noon and the trusses aren't here yet. Can you have the project manager call the truss company and find out what's going on?" That way, if it was known the trusses weren't going to be there, he could have adapted and kept the whole crew productive on days five and six with the next tasks with no lost production time.

And I stress this again: if someone gives you too many lame excuses why they can't get their job done, time after time, and the person never improves their performance no matter how much time you spend helping them, get rid of them. Put somebody in the position that will get the job done while taking pride in doing it. I am not saying that valid reasons don't happen that can cause problems and delays. I am talking about lame excuses.

Whether you realize it or not, you have a large amount of statistical info right in front of you.[2] How much did you spend with your individual suppliers per month last year? What was your payroll each month last year? What were your open contract values per month last year? How much did you deposit in the bank per month last year? How many new customers did you get? And the list goes on. You just take these values and put them on a graph by month for a year. You'll get a clear picture of what is going on and where you have to look to fix the problems.

Below are the key points outlining the administration of your company:

1. **HUMAN RESOURCES:** This includes hiring, pay scales, monitoring performance, evaluations, instruction, and matching people to their abilities. Do you have a good bunch of employees? Do you need more? Are you paying any of them too much or too little? Do you keep an eye on how well or how bad they do at their job? Do you give employee evaluations every six months or annually? As you know, the people you hire can make or break you. Unfortunately, there are rules that prevent you from asking certain questions on an application. But there is no rule that says you can't talk to the person and have a general conversation. Do background checks, certainly check references and give a drug test as part of the application.

   You can usually tell if you want to hire someone just by the way they fill out the application. If the person never stays in one spot for more than a year or so that sends up a red flag for me. If the person does not "remember" who his or her last supervisor was it tells me they didn't have enough attention on the structure of the company to care about doing a good job. Does the person answer the questions completely and fill in the information correctly? Can they spell? Can you read their writing? What is the person's appearance?

What are they asking for starting pay? And ask yourself these two questions: Will this person fit into the group? Do I want this person representing the company to my customers? If the answer is "no" to either one, this person is a no-hire. You want to hire people that will stay for the long haul, people you can work with and they with you to help you build the company.[3]

2.   **COMMUNICATIONS:** How is the mail, phone calls, and internet traffic handled when it comes in to the company? Do you have some sort of method in place to make sure all these communications get where they are supposed to go? How about going out of the company, how is that done? Is there an internal method of making sure the shop notifies production support when they are getting low on supplies and it is time to reorder? Is there someone in charge of all this? Do the section managers write memos to each other and if so how do they get where they are supposed to go? In this day and age, communication is very easy. Most businesses I know have a network where any employee can get the information they need off the server from their desktop, smartphone, or tablet. They communicate internally with e-mail. This is probably the most effective and timesaving way to keep everyone on the same page as long as everyone does it by the same policy.

3.   **MONITORING:** Do you walk around the company and check things out? Do you have a way to keep track of all the operations of the company? Do you keep any graphs of production and other key information that could help you find holes in the processes that are supposed to make things run smoothly and efficiently? Do you correct the things that you find? Is there someone in your company that monitors its areas and reports the findings to you? Chances are you have some system in place but is it working like it should?

Now let's put you to work on an exercise to help you organize this section and have some fun putting together the basics of administration to work in the company.

SUMMARY

There is so much information that goes along with this section that gigantic books have been written on each part. It is safe to assume those can be further study down the road if you so desire. We are sticking with the basics in this book. My goal is to give you what you need to get things on track to success.

Most likely you are beginning to see the whole picture here unfolding in front of you and are beginning to see the importance of being organized and aware of what is happening. You are starting to realize how all these areas rely on each other to make the operations run smoothly and perfectly and how the strength of the company relies on each and every person in it and what they do.

By organizing your activities, all these parts form a whole and work to complement each other. The more you do this the easier it will become and the more you will empower employees to hold the duties that you have been trying to hold all alone. Your duties will begin to become second nature, allowing you to free up your time, delegate responsibility, and correctly run your company or department, not have it run you.

CHAPTER TWO REFERENCES:

(1) The following references are from the Hubbard® Management System (HMS), which is based on the works of L. Ron Hubbard. These refences are additional information to help you understand the importance of statistics in your company. These are from Volume V entitled *Statistics Management*:

STATISTICS-WHAT THEY ARE

WHAT IS A *statistic*? A STATISTIC IS A NUMBER OR AMOUNT *compared* TO an earlier number or amount of the same thing. Statistics refer to the quantity of work done or the value of it in money.

A *down statistic* means that the current number is less than it was. An *up statistic* means the current number is more than it was.

Successful organizations and groups operate on statistics. These show whether or not a staff member or group is working or not working as the work produces the statistic. If he doesn't work effectively, the statistic inevitably goes down. If he works effectively, the statistic goes up.

STATISTICS AND PRODUCTS

ONE ALWAYS RUNS BY STATISTICS WHERE THESE ARE VALID.

Statistics must reflect actual desired PRODUCT. If they do not they are not valid. If they do, they give an idea of ideal scene.

From a statistic reflecting the desired products, one can work out the departure from the ideal scene.

A backlog of product production must reflect in a stat. As a backlog is *negative* production.

Every division is a production unit. It makes or does something that can have a statistic to see if it goes up or down.

Example: a typist gets out five hundred letters in one week. That's a statistic. If the next week the same typist gets out six hundred letters that's an UP statistic. If the typist gets out three hundred letters that's a DOWN statistic.

Every job in an organization can have a statistic. So does every portion of the organization.

The purpose is to keep production (statistics) up. This is the only thing that gives a good income.

When statistics go down or when things are so organized you can't get one for a Job, the organization goes down in its overall production.

The production of an organization is only the total of its individual employees. When these have down statistics so does the organization.

(2) Brad Efron, world renowned statistician says:

"*Those who ignore Statistics are condemned to reinvent it.*"

(3) Benjamin Franklin, American Inventor says:

"*He that is good for making excuses is seldom good for anything else.*"

Chapter Three

THE BASICS OF CLIENT MANAGEMENT

T he person or company that buys your products and services can be called a customer, client, patron, buyer, or consumer. All of these words have similar definitions. They just mean someone who buys something from someone. My personal favorite is *client* because the word inspires professionalism. You can call the people or companies that you do work for whatever you want, as long as that element of professionalism is practiced. Always keep in mind that these people and their organizations are the lifeblood and future of your business.

In this chapter we will look over and develop an understanding of how to organize the managing and keeping of your clients. First, we'll look over promotional and marketing principles and practices. Then we'll take up managing the client's journey into your company from an administrative service stand point. Lastly, in this chapter we'll cover what to do with all the information you gather on your clients and how it can be used to keep those clients coming back.

It holds true that in any business there are promotion and marketing requirements. You are, and have been, doing it to some degree whether you realize it or not. It can be done in many ways, some of them with blockbuster results and some not so much. You are in business and have been going along. You have clients that come and go. You also have clients that stick by your company to provide them with products and services on a repeat basis. But, why do some come and go and some remain loyal?

To clarify further, **promotion** is simply getting yourself, company, products, services, or business in the eyes of your clients on a continual basis. It is the actual compilation of the materials which contain a message about your company with a description of the product or service, your capability in providing it, and why the client should buy from or use you and/or your company.

The actions of individuals or the company as a whole are also a big part of promotion. That's right. Ever had a salesman come by inappropriately telling you about his company, begging for work? Just asking for sympathy because his company is near extinction? He won't leave you alone and although you remain respectful you fake a phone call just so you can ask him to leave. All of us have experienced some level of this I am sure. You would not have anything to do with him or his company. He is the representative of the company therefore the way he acts towards you definitely makes you develop an idea that there is something very wrong with that company. After all, he promoted that idea to you.

Therefore, your employees' appearance on the jobsite and how they communicate with workers from another trade or the client is promotion. It is these *actions* that *promote* the image and value of your company to others. If a client sees a smart-looking group, coordinated in their actions, they know there will be a job well done with no problems.

Marketing is the way that material is presented to and how it gets to the client. It is also the channels used to reach your target audience. For instance, if you made fish bowls and dog collars you wouldn't waste money marketing fish bowls to your clients who don't have any fish.

Alright then, what the hell is advertising? It is the actual message (promotion) targeted and delivered to the consumers of particular goods or services—marketing through any medium. A *medium* is the place you put your promotion, be it a newspaper, mailing, internet campaign, or the like. The important thing to know is that you have to make good promotional material and find your targeted market to advertise to.

To get an idea of how all this works, let's look at why you use a particular subcontractor or vendor. Let's say you use ABC Concrete exclusively for your footings, slab, and block work. Why? XYZ Concrete does the same type of work and their bid is lower, why not use them? Chances are ABC Concrete is in front of your face more. About once a month you get a newsletter from them, or an e-mail or even a visit from their sales rep. You are brought up to date on their successful projects, they have testimonials from clients, they tell you what equipment they've added to do a better job, and they ask questions about what type of projects you have coming up and how they can help.

As you look at these things you think, "Wow, now there is a professional company." You think about all the work they've done for your company and how well it turned out. You think about the people that work at or run ABC Concrete and how you have rarely had a problem with any of them, and the one or two times you did, it was solved easily and quickly with a phone call. So the next time you get a project you call them first. They give you an estimate for the job. You are able to discuss the job so that scheduling, material availability, and pricing are in line with the contract from your client and you are going to get concrete subcontracting *done* knowing that you will get a superb job, on time and within budget. You don't even ask any other concrete companies for an estimate because you know you are in good hands.

And that result is what promotion and marketing needs to accomplish for your business. What ABC Concrete has done is show their clients that they provide the best service and value for their clients, time after time.

There are a couple of steps you need to take to develop your skills so you know how to successfully market yourself. It's not difficult but it is rather precise.

The first things you need to know are: What do my clients want from a company that does what we do? What do my clients always need that is continually beneficial to them? How can I find this out?

There are very basic things you can do to gather the information you will need to do successful promotion and marketing:

- **LOOK AT YOUR OWN INVOICES TO CLIENTS: What do you see is the most repeated item or service that your clients continually get from you? If you are a plumbing contractor have you done the most work for new homes or remodels? Who were your clients? How many of them were repeat clients?**

- **LOOK AT YOUR COMPETITION: What do they do the most of? Let's say the company you own is Total Safe Alarm Service. Yet even in your own neighborhood you see signs on all your neighbor's lawns that say, "Protected by 24/7 Alarm Service." What do they provide that your company falls short on?**

- **LOOK AT TRADE AND INDUSTRY PUBLICATIONS: What is the biggest promotion in your industry or trade right now? What is coming in the future that you can prepare for and capitalize on so you are ready for when the industry advances?**

- **ASK YOUR CURRENT CLIENTS: What work are they doing that your company can provide support for? Where are they headed? What will they need or want in the future?**

As you can see we are talking here in this section only about your previous and present clients. We are looking at any clients your company has done work for thus far, since the day the company was formed and opened for business. This is your client base and is the heart of where all your company's sales and contracts has come from right up to this point in time.

* * *

The next part of this section is a very important action, **client orientation**. It is the experience you give your clients when they have contracted your company for services. The client has ended up continuing with or returned to using your company as a direct result of your promotion and marketing efforts. Nice!

Here is an example. Suppose your company is a steel fabricator and erector. Your client is a general contractor that has contracted you to provide the steel package for a three-story building. First, you want to find out what it is that makes the client continue to use your company; if they're a repeat client find out why they came back. If they're a new client, why did they choose your company this time? This is important statistical information that can be used in your promotion and marketing activities.

Next walk the client through your company and show how the company has become better than average by organizing its operations, what equipment has been added to provide steel components faster and more accurately, and any new services added since the last time the client used your company. Show the client projects you are currently working on. Answer any questions they may have about the operation.

The next step is to orient the client. Have a meeting with all the section managers in your company and the client's representatives. This is where the introduction to all your employees that will be responsible for the successful execution of the project happens with the client. This would include the client's project manager, safety manager, and field superintendent for the project at the very least.

Your client has to know who in your company is handling what area of the project from the receptionist right on through the individual sequences of section operations. The client has to have a direct contact with the person in your company that handles problems in the event they feel like they are not receiving the services they need, want, expect, or more importantly, were promised. Provided that all the employees do their jobs correctly, the person that handles these problems won't have to take any calls.

And remember what you are doing in these actions **is promotion.** Don't "spectacularize" things. Just give honest and straight answers. A person usually knows when you are feeding them crap. It just feels and tastes bad. You want just to show the path of the project as it flows through your organization with every step along that path addressed by a responsible employee in your company. Who they are, what their job title is, their experience in the industry, how long they have been with the company, and their contact info.

A general contractor expects kinks in the execution of a project. They mostly come from the owner of the project, architect, engineer, or the building department. You want to represent you and your company for what they can do and then prove it by doing it. Make it so your client knows they won't have any kinks with you and your company.

Let's put the shoe on the other foot. Your company is a general contractor and you have a three-story structural steel project that you are interviewing a sub-contractor for. You call three possible companies to set up a meeting with them to have a look at the project. The first company says, "Just send me the plans to bid on, that's all we need."

Second one says, "We don't give tours of our company operations."

Third one says, "We would be happy to show you around and have a look at your project."

The first one is out of the picture; they have no intention of servicing you properly to do a good job and keep you as a client. The second one is not a candidate because they are hiding something. For whatever reasons they are hiding their business, its structure, shop operations, their true capabilities and therefore, you are immediately uncertain whether or not they can do the project. Never enter into a contract with a company if you are uncertain right out of the gate. The third one opens up their doors and invites you to come on in and have a look. And there you go, interview them as a sub-contractor for your steel work.

You may get there and be totally convinced this is the steel company for your project. You may get there and be unimpressed with their organization and its operations and be fed a bunch of crap as well as immediately see that they could not handle the job. In which case keep on looking following what you now know on qualifying a sub-contractor.

As you can see the promotion element works both ways. Your company to your clients and your company *as a client*. Understanding this can help you avoid disaster and make it so you avoid dealing with any other service companies that have problems. All too often I have seen a contractor hire a sub-contractor that creates problems on a project, then doesn't finish the project or even files bankruptcy in the middle of it. Knowing what promotion is gives you a set of tools to recognize this beforehand and determine who to deal with and who not to deal with.

* * *

On to the last part of this section, client files. These would be the files on clients, past and present, in use for promotion and marketing. They would contain the client's business address, mailing address if different from physical address, website address, and phone and fax numbers, as well as e-mail for general contact. The file would also include all the people in that company that you and your company have ever dealt with, their positions, what their duties are, and their direct contact information. This is very important in your marketing. This should be kept in hard copy and in electronic format where you have the ability to select positions with certain duties to promote a specific thing to. Client files need to be kept up-to-date with all the correct information.[1]

These are not the same as the job or project files that you must keep by law on every project you have ever done for the respective client. Those files are project documents used to create the close-out and turnover package for the project. More about those later on.

Let's say your company is a framing contractor and your company just added their own crane to its equipment list. This now means that you don't have to hire and depend on a crane service to put up the roof trusses on the projects you do. Not being able to get a crane when you need it is never a problem again. This is a big advancement in a positive direction for your company and it puts you a cut above all other framing contractors in the area.

The first thing you do is go to your client files and find the person in every client's company who has ever hired your company to do framing work and market to them the fact you now have your own crane.

This shows your client two things: your company invests in itself and your company is interested in, and takes pride in, providing a service superior to the "other guy." Professionalism is your friend. It speaks volumes. It is the primary action for success.

If you sent the communication generally, it would of course do no good, or be seen as junk mail for the garbage can and may never reach the proper person. You have just wasted time and money by not marketing your promotion correctly. You want to market your promotion directly to the person in charge of that activity you support.

You are probably wondering, "OK, this is how I take care of clients I have already done business with. What about new clients?" There is an entire future chapter in this book that covers new business. These same basic principles and practices will hold true in that chapter as well, to a very marked degree.

Below are the key points outlining how to deal with client management:

1. **PROMOTION AND MARKETING:** This consists of promotional materials that you market to your repeat clients. It contains the up-to-date report of your company showing what you have always done, what you have added to better serve your clients, any new employees and their experience and credentials and what they bring to the company, and new services and equipment. Start taking pictures and videos of everything that is done in the company. You will need any and all visual representations of what you do to properly assemble all your promotion. It can be a postcard, newsletter, or internet campaign. It gets sent directly to that person in your client's company who is responsible for making the business decision for that service.

2. **CLIENT ORIENTATION:** This is how you treat your client. Be an open house for your client. This is the coming together of your company and your client's company, with attention paid to all the details of all the people involved in the activity. Make sure that each person understands the functions of the other people on both sides. You are creating an environment where both companies are able to communicate and support one another.

3.   **CLIENT FILES:** These are your permanent records on each of your clients that gives you a marketing channel to send your company promotion to. It is important that you have all the information on each of your clients.[2] For some reason, some companies and individuals will fall into the category of those you would rather not do business with anymore. Always keep your client files complete and up-to-date. Then you will not make waste marketing to a non-client.

And now it is time to update your organizational chart for this section.

EXERCISE: FILL IN THE CLIENT SECTION ON THE CHART.

Go back to the chart you made and list the three key points of client manage-ment, in order from top to bottom, in the third column under "Sales Manager." Just like you have been doing, leave space between each key point and in that space list out all the things that are done to make each point a reality in your company. List the functions that are performed and who does them.

SUMMARY

Unless you have been sleeping (which I seriously doubt), you will have noticed that **"you"** has been the operative word in the description of every duty. Well, I am sorry to have to tell you, if you are the leader, no matter who actually does the work, the responsible party is you.

If you are the owner and the sole person trying to build a company, it is also you. If there is no one else but you in the company then you have to do all of it. Just because it's your responsibility, though, doesn't mean you should be doing everything; it's important to make a plan, follow the plan, and teach your employees to follow the plan and show your clients that the company follows a plan.

As you put all this together from a leadership position, make sure that the duties, organization, and business-building you are creating from these chapters are assigned to the employees in those sections where they are implemented and executed.

You are not creating more work for yourself here. You are creating an organization composed of a group of people working together to forward the ideals, goals, and purposes of the company as a whole. Allow the employees of the company to create like you do.

CHAPTER THREE REFERENCES:

(1) Policy 18 November 1969 CENTRAL FILES, VALUE OF THE GROSS INCOME OF THE ORG AND WHY BY L. Ron Hubbard.

Mr. Hubbard says:

"An org's potential fortune, its potential gross income is its CF."

"Listen: There is no other route to gross income than via CF."

(Org is short for organization)

(CF stands for Central Files in this reference)

(2) Greg Thaler, internationally known forensic accountant says:

"Contact data ages like fish not wine...it gets worse as it gets older, not better."

THE BASICS OF COMPANY FINANCE

F inance is simply the management of the money or credit resources of a company or individual.

In the first part of this chapter I will review the income of the company and how it is used as the fuel to keep the company going and growing. The next part covers how you pay the company's bills. In the last part you'll see the record-keeping aspect of it all, as well as preserving your assets through proper allocation of money for the future.

But first, let's look at what **money** really is. Money is a guaranty that you accept, in the form of printed paper or coin in exchange for goods or services provided, with the idea that the money will be honored to buy other goods or services.[1] That's really all it is.

It began its use to take the place of trading with goods and services. Let's say you wanted to trade your cow for ten bales of hay you needed to feed the horses. You brought your cow to the local hay farmer, but he didn't want a cow. The hay farmer knew a guy who wanted a cow about four miles north and that guy had a plow hitch that the hay farmer needed. So now you have to make an eight-mile round trip, four miles of it with the cow and the other four miles with the plow hitch. You then trade the hay farmer for the ten bales of hay. After you went around the countryside for two days you made it home. Tough break.

Someone came up with the idea of money so all that didn't have to happen. You could give the hay farmer money for the ten bales of hay. You wouldn't have to go roaming around the countryside trading your stuff for other stuff until you could get what you wanted. Life got easier.

This created a whole new landscape. Single stores, carrying any and all the goods one would ever need, began to spring up in a central location of the community. Store keepers began to find out they had to sell the goods at a higher price to the buyer in order to pay expenses for the store, the help, goods going bad before they were sold, damage, theft, and whatever else happened in those days. And profit had to be made so the store owner could afford to buy land, build a house, feed his family, and build the business to meet more demands of existing and increasing numbers of consumers.

Enter in banks. A safe place to store the money you took in until you needed it again to pay for more goods, services, and expenses. Yup, that is the original reason banks were formed. A small fee kept your money safe. Not so much today.

Fast forward to today and what do we have? Plastic money, electronic money, loans, credit cards, interest, and of course profit or loss. But enough with the history lesson.

INCOME

What you must know is that your company receives money for providing services or delivering products to your clients at a rate sufficient enough to be stable and keep growing.

The leader of a company must know how much it costs the business to provide its products and services in exchange for money from the client. This includes a lot of information you need to know in order to charge a sufficient amount for what you do. It is also necessary to have enough money to put aside for when times are rough, cover your accounts receivable, to pay for borrowed money, replace equipment when it gets worn out or breaks, and the one that most business owners forget, operating capital.

Operating capital is that amount of money that you have in the bank that is not connected to any bills, debt, expenses, or other financial obligations of any kind. It is money that is usually used for financing projects that have a time period between when the company performs the service and when the client pays for that service. It can be used for other purposes as long as what you spend it on generates its return, plus profit.

You must know how much it costs to provide products and services to the client. Every penny from everywhere. I can't stress the importance of knowing this enough! You have no choice but to understand all the relative and associated costs of the company in delivering the finished product or performing its services if you expect to be successful.

I met an electrical contractor one time that was trying to sell his business. They did about $5M a year in income. They kept minimum books on the finances. No one was interested in the business after looking at the financial records because there was no way of telling if the business made any money. Of course, the owner said he made a ton of money because he believed it and there was no way to disprove it. He lived like a king.

So, he had his staff spend the next three months reviewing and correcting the finances from top to bottom. You know what he learned? The business was not making any money, but in fact, had been barely floating along … for years. He could not sell it in that condition.

You are going to need to know how much all your business expenses cost every month. Every penny you spend to open the company doors every morning. Gather up the past four months because every month is going to vary a little bit. Find the average cost per month. Make sure you include everything. If you buy flowers for the reception area once a week, include those too. Below is an example monthly expense spreadsheet.

MONTHLY EXPENSE SUMMARY					
ITEM	January	February	March	April	AVERAGE
Rent/Mortgage	1,200	1,200	1,200	1,200	1,200
Electric/Phone/Internet/Utilities	353	331	404	316	351
Water/Sewer/Trash	185	185	185	185	185
Vehicles/Equipment/Tools	884	689	977	714	816
Office Supplies/Equipment	188	183	211	187	192.25
Taxes/Insurance	300	300	300	300	300
Miscellaneous	154	149	201	111	153.75
Cleaning/Maintenance	160	160	160	160	160
TOTALS	3,424	3,197	3,638	3,173	3,358

As you can see, at this company it costs an average of $3,358.00 per month to keep the doors open. This does not include the labor for the office employees or any associated costs for labor like insurances, income taxes, paid days off or vacations, or any other labor burden. This is the cost of your office, shop, or whatever facility you have and will be unique to it. I have found that Microsoft Excel is the most user-friendly program for these spreadsheets. You should teach yourself how to use it if you don't already know how or get someone to train you.

Now take a look at what your labor and associated costs add up to in order to keep every employee paid for your regular work week. You have to figure in paid days off, vacation time, sick days, bonuses, workers comp insurance, commercial liability, and federal and state income taxes. Even include company Christmas parties, Friday pizza, or anything else you do for all the employees. Below is an example labor spreadsheet.

MONTHLY LABOR SUMMARY					
ITEM	January	February	March	April	AVERAGE
1 Owner/CEO	7,500	7,500	7,500	7,500	7,500
2 Office Employees	4,000	4,000	4,000	4,000	4,000
1 Warehouse Employee	3,000	3,000	3,000	3,000	3,000
2 Installers	12,000	12,000	12,000	12,000	12,000
Overtime Pay	1,120	0	560	328	502
Vacation/Paid Off Days	846	846	846	846	846
Income Tax/Social Security/Medicare	500	500	500	500	500
Workers Comp/Health Insurance	1,741	1,448	1,592	1,515	1,574
Bonuses	200	0	100	72	93
Other Employee Benefits	155	155	155	155	155
MONTHLY TOTAL	31,062	29,294	30,098	29,761	30,015

You add the average **Monthly Expense Summary** amount, $3,358, and the average **Monthly Labor Summary** amount, $30,015, which equals $33,373, to find out the least amount the company needs to make to break even every month.

Now, break it down to how much every hour for every person in the company costs on average. The spreadsheet below shows the average monthly total divided by the number of employees, including the owner (six total in this example), and that amount divided by the average number of work hours in a month, which is 172 per person.

Now take the average monthly total	**30,015**
Divided by six paid employees equals	5,003
Divided by 172 average hours per month gives average dollars per hour labor cost complete with all associated expenses	**$29.09**

So, now you have to establish your company's hourly billable labor rate for services. It obviously has to be higher than what the labor costs are, because some form of billable production has to pay for the actual physical location of the business and the operations performed there to produce your products and services for your clients.

Let's say you bring your car in for repairs to the local garage. There is a sign on the wall that says "Labor Rate = $65.00 per hour." That is the garage's billable labor rate. That is the rate you get charged for every hour the mechanic works on your car. If it is a tough job requiring two mechanics, then it will be $65.00 X 2 = $130.00 per hour multiplied by how many hours it takes them.

And why do we need a billable labor rate for the whole company? Because not all employees directly produce the product or service to the client. For instance, there is a bookkeeper, receptionist, and warehouse person. They get paid but they don't directly do work for a client, even though the employees or technicians that do work directly for the client could not do their jobs without them or their support.

Next we are going to breakdown the Monthly Expense Summary into cost per hour and add it to the hourly labor costs from the Monthly Labor Summary. On the next page is what that looks like, in an example spreadsheet, using all of what we have calculated so far.

Take the average monthly expense	3.358
Divide by the average 172 hours in a month for hourly expense cost	$19.53
Added to the hourly labor cost	29.09
Subtotal	48.62
Plus standard profit on labor 10%	4.86
Gives your labor rate per hour	53.08
Round up for billable labor rate	$54.00

You now know how to calculate how much the billable labor rate for your company must be. If you are charging less than what it should be, you are giving money away. If you are charging too much more than what it should be, you will price yourself right out of work. Now, realize that when your company has a better reputation and track record for doing great work on time, you are in a position higher than your competition, and you can charge a little bit more. Don't gouge your clients though, because they'll go to the next guy in line. Remember, professionalism is extremely important. Promote it always.

If your current labor rate is lower, then you have to raise it to what you discovered it needs to be. If its higher, and you are still competitive, leave it alone. Well done on your part. You can base your labor rate on what the competition charges, you just damn well better be sure it is sufficient to allow you to keep your company going and growing.

Here is an example of how to figure out what to charge for your services. Let's look at an example of ABC landscape company hired to landscape a new home.

First, take the plans, count up all the plant types and get all the plants priced up from the supplier. Any of the materials and supplies that you will be using to get the project done have to be counted.

Then, take the plans to your project manager (or estimator) and have them work out how long it will take, with how many employees, what type of rental equipment, needed supplies, company vehicles and equipment, etc. If you don't have these employees, then get with your best installer and sit and work out these things with him. He's in the field doing the work so he'll know what it will take to get the job done.

List all these things on a spreadsheet to get your costs plus a 25 percent profit on the whole job. Below is an example spreadsheet for this.

EXAMPLE HOME LANDSCAPE PROJECT			
ITEM	Quantity	Cost Each	Total
Plants/Flowers	17	$12.00	$204.00
Shrubs	11	$31.00	$341.00
Trees	9	$77.00	$693.00
Timbers	112	$5.00	$560.00
Fill Dirt, Yards	44	$10.50	$462.00
Rock, Yards	33	$90.00	$2,970.00
Rented Equipment (Bobcat Dozer)	1	$1,288.00	$1,288.00
Company Tools/Vehicles/Equipment	1	$210.00	$210.00
Administrative Labor, Hours	8	$54.00	$432.00
On Site/Warehouse Labor, Hours	100	$54.00	$5,400.00
	Cost Total		$12,560.00
	25% Profit		$3,140.00
	Total Proposal Amount		**$15,700.00**

I am fairly certain you have begun to get a grip on how to make sure your company charges a fair price for the production of its products and services to a client. These values can vary from industry to industry, but this is a general rule of thumb. Remember, all these numbers and values are all just made up to show you the basic formulas of how to accomplish these actions so you gain a firm understanding of basic finance.

OK. You have a project that will take two installers about a week to do, along with one day for administration and two and a half days for the warehouse person. Let's do a little more work, using this project example, to find out how many of these size projects ABC landscape company has to do a month to make it all worthwhile.

You can't count everything in the proposal because a lot of the costs have to do with just this job. Because each project has its own materials connected with it, you would not count those. The only thing you would count is the billable labor for the simple reason it is the only action which reflects production and *only* production equals income through billable hours in a service business. Add all the administrative and production labor together for the project, and that total labor adds up to be $5,832.

You know that in this example the company costs $33,373 on average to keep the doors open per month. Divide that $33,373 by the labor amount on this example project, $5,832, and that equals roughly six projects of this size which must be done every month for the company to keep going and growing.

I can hear you wondering, "But what about the 10 percent profit on labor and the 25 percent profit on the project cost total?" You are very sharp to have spotted this.

Earlier in this chapter you read about keeping the company going and **growing** and about **enough money to have some to put aside for when times are rough, cover your accounts receivable, to pay for borrowed money, replace equipment when it gets worn out or breaks, and the one that most business owners forget, operating capital..**

That is what that part of your company's money is for. Plain and simple. Operating capital is that money the company uses to finance projects or accounts receivable over time. Without it, the company works from hand to mouth; it never grows.

PAYING THE BILLS

This is where I see the biggest mishandling of money, so I am going to talk about this a little bit to show you what this looks like.

In any industry, we have clients who pay up front and this is good because you have the money right now to pay for the materials and labor right away. There is no future debt connected with the project if you pay as you go. Although this is the ideal scenario, it will not be the majority of your clients if you are going to do standard work as a contractor. You will have to play by different rules than this to play a bigger game.

Consider the following: there are clients who have a credit account that use your company's services for a month, then you send them a statement at the end of the month, and then they have anywhere from five to thirty days to pay, which means you are financing their work for up to sixty days.

Then there is the contract method where you enter into and sign an agreement with a contractor that your company sub-contracts to. This works much the same as the above credit account client, but as you may know, this is performance based. That means you only get paid for the part of the project you have completed for the month. This is usually a large project that you will be on for a month or more. If there are delays by weather, or other kinks, there may be little or nothing to collect for the month, because although your crews are working on it, you haven't completed a billable phase. This means another month goes by that your company spends money without collecting any.

These two scenarios, where your company waits for the income, is where the trouble begins. Because it is your company's financial strength that keeps the client's project moving, money tends to come from places it shouldn't to keep the project on track or keep production rolling at all within the company—robbing from Peter to pay Paul.

In other words, using the money from one project to pay for another project. In some states this is actually a violation of construction law as established by the Department of Business and Professional Regulations.

Accounts receivable is money you are waiting to collect for work your company has already done. Your company basically finances the project.

Accounts payable is the money you owe your suppliers and every other expense it takes to keep those doors open and the company producing each and every month.

It doesn't matter whether you collect on the accounts receivable or not, the accounts payable has to be paid every month. **And that is another action point of promotion.** If your company does not pay its bills as agreed, eventually no other company will deal with you, including your clients.

There are ways to finance projects in addition to using the company's operating capital which include: loans, credit cards, and even companies that will buy your accounts receivable to give you operating capital.

The point here is, pay all the bills for the project with the money you collect from the project. That includes any and all money you borrowed to finance the project. It includes putting the operating capital back in its hiding spot. If you do that then you will be in good shape. If you don't do that and you allow the mismanagement of the money, there will come a day, sooner or later, where you won't be opening the doors for business.

You need an allocation plan which is followed to properly allocate every single dollar you collect, to the correct expenses, by the week.

An *allocation* is simply the setting aside of money for its specific purpose and not using it for anything but its specific purpose.

Why is this done by the week? Because all the bills do not come on the same day. Some are due on the fifth, some on the tenth, some on the fifteenth, and so on and so forth.

Plus you will collect and bank your income by the week, especially with pay-as-they-go clients. You will also have client credit accounts and contract payments that get received each week as well.

Based on what you have learned so far, you can see how this all fits together. The dos and the don'ts, and why you do and why you don't. If someone would've had the graces to tell me all this when I first started all those many years ago, I would have been very thankful.

Making an allocation plan is easier than you may think. Yep, you guessed it: another simple spreadsheet. This is how you program your bills or payments to be paid on time.

If the ABC landscape company completes and gets paid for all six projects in the same month this is easy. The money collected goes in the bank and when your bills come due you pay them on time. What you do is allocate the money and *don't spend that money on anything else.* You keep it in your company checking account and it is there for when you get the bills connected with the jobs and to run the business. Then the bills get paid on time.

If you use QuickBooks or another accounting program it can even do this for you.

From the Example Home Landscape Project spreadsheet, we multiply the price of the job, $15,700, by the number of jobs (six), which equals $94,200 in the bank. It would look like the spreadsheet below filled in with all the dollar amounts from all the previous calculations we've done so far.

ABC LANDSCAPE COMPANY		
INCOME ALLOCATION		**FEBRUARY 20XX**
DEPOSITED IN BANK	$94,200.00	**INCOME BALANCE**
Amount Due Suppliers	$28,765.00	
		$65,435.00
Amount Due for Facility Costs	$3,358.00	
		$62,077.00
Average Monthly Labor Costs	$30,015.00	
		$32,062.00
Additional Overtime Labor Costs	$2,013.00	
		$30,049.00
Rental Equipment Amount	$7,084.00	
		$22,965.00
Company Equipment Costs	$1,155.00	
		$21,810.00
10% Profit on Labor	$2,970.00	
		$18,840.00
25% Profit on Each Job	$18,840.00	
		$0.00

There you go. As you can see, everything is paid for and the company is sitting on a total profit of $21,810 for the month. Not too shabby, is it? Now, we are going to do just one more spreadsheet to show the possibilities of allocation for the profit.

A mistake you don't want to make is to spend money on a promise. If the money is not in the bank, don't spend it. I have seen people take the promise of a contract and spend the value of the contract on something, then never get the contract. Ouch!

Your company would be well served to use a bookkeeper on a regular basis. If there is one in the company that is great. The information in this chapter will serve in helping the bookkeeper understand what plan the company is following. The objective here is to give you the basic tools to develop that plan for your company.

Use an accountant for taxes and other major finance tasks. Your company should have both to keep all this straight.

Here is what that profit allocation spreadsheet may look like. The beauty of this is that this money belongs to the company and any of the values can be changed to better serve the needs of the company for expansion purposes.

ABC LANDSCAPE COMPANY			
PROFIT ALLOCATION		**FEBRUARY 20XX**	
PROFIT AMOUNT	$21,810.00	INCOME BALANCE	
Promotion and Marketing	$1,527.00		
		$20,283.00	
Facility Improvements	$2,181.00		
		$18,102.00	
Facility Repairs	$2,181.00		
		$15,921.00	
Vehicle Maintenance & Repairs	$1,091.00		
		$14,830.00	
New Vehicles	$2,181.00		
		$12,649.00	
Equipment & Tools	$2,181.00		
		$11,588.00	
Operating Capital	$9,377.00		
		$9,377.00	
		$0.00	

Another benefit of this practice is that if anything unforeseen occurs, it won't cripple the company. There is money to fall back on when kinks occur.

As you work with this plan you can see how you could break this down by weekly income and bill payments. The more you use it, the easier it will become and the better decisions you'll make to benefit the growth of the company. If you're delegating this task to an employee, make sure that they know these formulas and use them.

This format is, by far, not the only one in existence. I can testify under oath, however, that this works and produces the expected results 100 percent of the time. I have used it time and again rescuing companies from ashes.

Before we go on to the last part of this section I want to share with you a piece of knowledge about expanding a business that you will find very helpful. Do not expand faster than your company has the resources to support. As you have seen, or knew already, there are many ways to finance projects. Done on a scale which allows the company to grow, one can make the company strong and as big as they want. Done too quickly, you're headed for disaster.

Case in point: Many years ago, I worked with a company that was doing several million a year income, with about fifty employees and projects averaging about 300 to 500 thousand each. They did excellent work, paid their bills on time, and provided their employees with health insurance and bonuses. The company had money in the bank, an A+ credit rating, was adding new equipment to expand its services, and was a model company as well as an industry leader. All was good and they were going and growing very nicely.

The company then signed a multi-million-dollar contract, carrying huge penalties for lack of performance and late completion. The timeline to do the project was physically impossible. Although it was a two-year project, the company promised completion in a year and made the grave mistake of basing its proposal on that one year. Right out of the gate, the dollar value for the contract was about four million less than it should have been because the labor costs were based on one year and added time means added equipment, expenses, and associated costs.

In an effort to perform, the company way overextended its ability to finance the project, piling up huge debt it could not repay. Because there was a lack of equipment, finance, and correct supervision as well as the lack of sufficient labor forces, the company could not keep up with the performance-driven schedule and thus could not get paid regularly. The company began to creak on its foundation.

Other work and existing clients that were serviced perfectly, prior to this, suffered. Adequate income dwindled. Otherwise loyal clients found other contractors. Several years later the company was still not paying their bills, had two rounds of layoffs, and still did not regain its once shining reputation in the industry. They just couldn't turn it around.

Why? They took a project that was way too big for their resources. *Resources* being the amount of money or credit they can afford to finance the project, the equipment necessary to fulfill the needs of the project, and the number of employees needed to perform the work on the project.

So, you have to be very confident in your company's ability to handle a project larger than they are used to. I cannot make that determination for you, but I can give you an idea of what it looks like on paper. The ultimate decision is from the kingpin of the company.

On the next page is a chart. It shows an "operating zone" for a company's project dollar amount that it successfully performs over a period of time. The dotted lines on the graph show the high and low dollar range of normal projects. This is the successful range the company operates in every month year after year. It is a nice upward trend of growing. It is the ideal condition for the company to continue going and growing. It can be exceeded, provided the company has the resources to perform projects of a value that it can support.

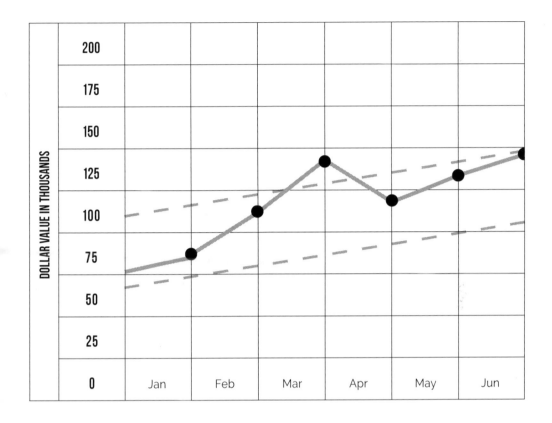

As in the example above, done right, you can exceed the operating zone and end up back in it. Your next six months will push that operating zone (the area between the dotted lines) into a higher range. Your company is growing.

In the graph below, you see what happens if the ability of the company resources cannot support the dollar value in projects.

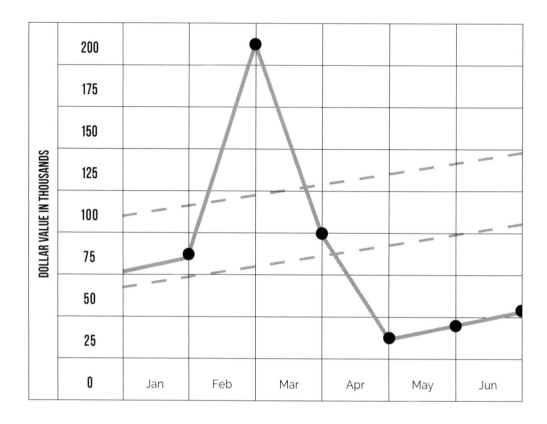

As in the example above, done wrong, you could greatly exceed the operating zone and end up way below it. Because the resources of the company were not sufficient at the time the project was taken, it cost the company far and above what it should have. It had to turn regular projects and clients away because it just didn't have the resources to perform those regular projects in the time frame needed. It lost one or more of its regular clients because they went to the competitor. Your next six months will push that operating zone into a *lower* range. Your company is *shrinking*.

Now, there are ways to take a job far outside your company's operating zone and end up back in it. I have done it and won a few times. My favorite was a very high-profile public project that was in great danger of going into default. I got called in to rescue it. The project was 1200 miles from our facility. It was about four times above the operating zone of my company at the time.

I negotiated with the company I was contracted with to pay the billable labor rate, materials, equipment, supplies, and expenses for the project by the week, by bank wire. I just made it perfectly clear that they were financing the project, not me and not our company. That way I paid every bill every week and did not incur any debt on the project.

I hired twenty-two people just for that project and it in no way affected the company's existing projects, employees, clients, or the production facility. It worked out win-win for both companies. It was one of those extreme luck, once-in-a-lifetime deals.

Risks are a part of any industry. Having this information can help one better evaluate the amount of risk the company can be exposed to and continue going and growing.

RECORD KEEPING AND ASSET PRESERVATION

Alright, on to the last part of this section which is record keeping and asset preservation. This is a very important and often overlooked part of business.

Are all your company's financial records in order? Can you quickly lay your hands on your company's tax returns, payroll records, insurance policies, client project files, and supplier files? All these need to be in order, correct, and up-to-date.

As you grow the company you may be subject to audits. An audit is an official examination and verification of accounts and records, especially of financial accounts. It can be done by various entities for many purposes, with taxes and insurances being the most common. If all your ducks are in a row, an audit is nothing to be afraid of and will show whomever is doing it that you and the company take care of business properly.

Does your company have a complete file on each and every piece of equipment, vehicles, power tools, hand tools, and stocked items (inventory), as well as the building and its improvements? Every one of these items has a value that contributes to the worth of the business. You have to know that worth and whether it is staying the same, increasing, or decreasing. Another bit of statistical information for you to look at and correct if necessary.

If you seek credit to expand, the creditor will want the combined value of these items for several reasons. By just these assets alone a bank can tell if you are operating the business correctly. The bank uses that statistical information to see if you are investing back into the company by adding equipment to increase client services, labor forces to provide more services to more clients, and the company's ability to handle larger projects as well as more of them.

In other words, let's say you started a company providing welding services. Ten years ago you took your life savings of $50,000 and spent it on everything you needed. It was you, a truck, and the equipment in that truck to do mobile welding. If in ten years it's still just you and that same truck and equipment, now older and more worn out, then the company will only be worth about 10 percent of what the value of everything was, or about $5,000. You are not likely to get credit for your company because there really is no company, it's just you working to earn a living.

On the other hand, if you started the same way and you followed the principles and practices from this chapter, let's see what ten years later could look like. Now the company has ten mobile welding trucks, its own fabricating facility, forty employees, money in the bank, very small debt, and has an income of $3 million a year. The company is now worth $3 million minimum plus whatever the value of the assets are. Creditors will stand in line to give you money. You have proven that you can run a business and manage the money profitably while doing it.

This chapter has covered a lot of ground. You see how sufficient income is directly related to fixed costs for everything connected with the business. You would be unable to see the importance of sufficient income without first establishing what that income needs to be.

This is why the cost of doing business and income are comingled in this chapter. I will further separate out the parts of this section into their key points below. An important basic concept to remember is that you need to have a handle on the finances of your company. The money it makes is the energy which fuels it today and a future of tomorrows.

Below are the key points outlining the finances of your company:

1.   **INCOME:** Make sure that you are charging your clients the correct rates for the products and services the company provides. What does your company's income need to be based on its expenses to operate? What is the labor rate your company has to charge hourly to support the payroll for the entire company? How much does the company need in income to keep going and growing? What is the income of the company right now?

I have seen companies that have not been charging adequate labor rates have trouble keeping up with the rising costs of all their expenses. You see their once shining trucks go to ruins, their employees in old t-shirts instead of company uniforms, and their shop equipment broken down for lack of maintenance funds.

2.   **BILLS:** The company needs to have a schedule of bills, vendor, and supplier invoices kept up-to-date with when they are due and what they are for. Do you review your invoices to make sure the amounts are correct? Are the bills paid on time? On time means by the due date, not necessarily when you receive it. You can pay bills and invoices the day you receive them, but that will not benefit your account status. Keep the company's money in the bank account as long as possible; maintaining a high account balance will benefit you. Only pay bills by the due date.

Most people just look at the bottom line and pay it. Do *not* operate that way. I have found supplier invoices riddled with mistakes and overages. I am not talking about little mistakes either. Always check to make sure the invoice you're paying matches the estimate you received for whatever it is you purchased.

3.   **RECORDS:** Keeping accurate financial, inventory, ownership, and service records of every asset of the company is paramount. Any asset that is not properly cared for becomes a liability. *Assets* are those items, facilities, machines, equipment, or tools that serve a purpose which returns a valuable benefit. *Liabilities* are those same things but in disrepair, always costing the company ridiculous amounts of time and money, with very little or even no valuable benefit.

Case in point: A company buys a $50,000 service truck. It's the company's newest asset. Nobody keeps track of when the oil change is due or even the oil level in the engine. 30,000 miles go by and the oil never gets checked or changed. The engine blows up. The truck is now a liability. It cost $10,000 for a new engine and three weeks of down time. But there were projects it was booked on. Do the projects get delayed? Not hardly, unless you want to lose clients. So now you have to rent a truck. More money, more time, the liability increases. It is a pretty unbelievable sight to watch this happen and even more startling when one witnesses the amount of time and money spent to correct what could have easily been avoided.

Proper maintenance of assets means fewer repairs, more service time, and preservation of the value of those assets. This takes a little time and effort and is the responsibility of every employee.

OK. Now it is time to get to work on your chart again.

EXERCISE: FILL IN THE FINANCE SECTION ON THE CHART.

Go back to the chart you made and list the three key points of finance, in order, top to bottom, in the fourth column under "Finance Manager." Just like you have been doing, leave space between each key point and in that space list out all the things that are done to make each point a reality in your company. List the functions that are performed and who does them.

SUMMARY

The financial aspect of any industry has normal operating guidelines. Know your industry and calculate the profit accordingly. Different industries have different profit margins. Smaller jobs may bring 25 percent profit, larger jobs 10 percent profit and emergency jobs 50 percent or higher.

This chapter covers the service industry. If your company doesn't do service but instead manufactures machines or some type of completed product, the formulas here still apply. What does it cost your company in time and material to build each item? What is the profit you get in each item? You would use the same format as covered here.

As you practice the principles of this chapter you'll see things come together like magic. There are going to be all sorts of things you'll discover. I know of at least one manager that found a bookkeeper taking small amounts of money for herself every week. Not enough to notice per week, but when added up over the years she was there, it was a couple hundred thousand dollars! She was definitely a liability!

Again, I will say, pick out the employees in charge of this section and make them responsible for their part of it. As the leader you should teach and coach and watch what is being done and make sure it is done correctly and completely.

And always remember, the employees of the company are its living assets. Without them there would be no company. If you find an employee that is a liability, do whatever can be done to help them become an asset. If that does not work, remove them. They will cause too much heartache to the other living assets and the future of your company.

CHAPTER FOUR REFERENCES:

(1) Policy 27 November 1971 Issue I, MONEY written by L. Ron Hubbard.

Mr. Hubbard says:

"Basically *money* is 'an idea backed by confidence'."

. . .

"So MONEY is only something that can be exchanged confidently for goods or services. It is a symbol that represents value in terms of goods and services."

. . .

"Money is simply that which represents delivered production."

Chapter Five

THE BASICS OF PRODUCTION

N ow it is time to have a look at the company's production. There are three sections to the production/delivery area of a company that provides products and/or services to their clients. You have undoubtedly seen these sections on the chart you have been filling in as part of the exercises throughout this book. Now, let's dive right in here and get to it.

So, what is **production?** It is the actions that create something of value. Therefore, it is what every employee is or should be doing as their duties to make the company operate in the production and delivery area, creating a sufficient income to keep it going and growing.

And what is *delivery?* It is the transferring of those things of value, which make up a project or phase of it, over to the client, getting the company paid for its production.

It is easy to see that producing things doesn't necessarily mean they get delivered. How many times have you been to a store looking for something and the slot where that item is supposed to be is empty? Way up on the top shelf are several huge boxes of the product you need. And as much as you want to, based on getting yelled at before, you don't climb the shelves to get it yourself. You get aggravated at the time it is going to cost you to get what you need. What would have been a simple in and out exercise is now going to delay your production schedule, even if it's just honey-do day around the house.

Now you have to find someone who works there to get one of those orange or blue rolling metal stairs and go up and get the thing you need. And much to your surprise he goes up the stairs and gets *only* the one you need! He leaves the point of sale slot empty!

Production is happening because you can see all those big boxes full of merchandise. Delivery is not happening efficiently because you cannot get the product easily.

This chapter covers several key points of production and delivery: production support, which includes asset maintenance and repair, shop production, and field (jobsite) production/delivery. Although we have looked at asset maintenance and repair in Chapter 1 as one of the key points of ownership and Chapter 4 as one of the key points of finance, this section is where the actual actions are performed to maintain and repair the company's assets.

These three sections work very closely with one another to make work happen, keep production occurring smoothly and efficiently, and honor the client's needs and wants while delivering to the client, on time and within budget, a better-than-expected result.

First, let's look at **production support**. Making sure that each area of production is supported properly is a major concern for the success of any business. It is the backup that production receives that determines if the products and services are completed on time as well as those production actions occurring in an efficient manner with superior results.

Let's take a company that makes pencils. At first, one would think "Well, it's just a pencil," but let's look at what it really means. In that pencil there is graphite, wood, metal, an eraser, and paint. Where do these things come from, and who buys them? Are you getting these items in house on time? Is the best price and delivery schedule being attained? Who receives them and confirms the delivery matches what was ordered? Is the raw material of the quality necessary? How do the raw materials get to the production line? Is each machine that performs a function in producing a pencil operating correctly? Have those machines been serviced on time? Are they kept in good repair? And on and on and not one pencil has been made yet. All these things and more must be done in order for the production area to make "just a pencil."

In the service industry, such as construction or its contractor trades, it gets way more intricate with many more moving parts contributing to the time and effort of production.

Take a company that does fabrication and erects structural steel. Here is a bit of a challenge to organize and support because both shop and field operations are required to do the project. For the shop there has to be detailed fab drawings made from the construction documents. The material needs to be brought in, personnel assigned, various processing equipment scheduled, and a production schedule needs to be made. All the shop equipment has to be fully maintained and functional. All the usable supplies in stock for the project must be identified. Long lead items and special operations must be predicted to fully coincide with the schedule. Final coating of primer or galvanizing must be entered into the timeline. And then there is delivery to the jobsite in sequence of erecting. Notice this is all planning and not one piece of steel has been fabricated yet. Who does all this?

Now let's go to the jobsite. There has to be erection drawings covering all the pertinent details, sequence, finished elevations, and any special items. A survey is needed on the jobsite to make sure that anchor bolts are in the right spot and at the correct elevation, wall placement is per plans, and any space or height restrictions that would affect erection procedures are noted. The rented equipment such as a Lull (extended reach all-terrain forklift) or crane has to be on site at the proper time. All the company-supplied equipment such as field service trucks, tools, manpower, and any other applicable supplies or devices to perform the operations have to be assigned.

All the contact info for the jobsite personnel needs to be provided as well as portable toilets and dumpsters for the crew. On projects where travel is required rooms need to be booked, travel arrangements made, and a means to obtain supplies established in that city. Who does all this?

The employees that make up the production support do all this. Production support's job is to make sure that every base is covered so no kinks occur.

It's all too common to hear a shop foreman or field foreman complain about not getting support, or that he or she has to do "everything around here." If you've ever been on a construction site, you've probably heard about or observed this from other trades. You've possibly heard it from your own employees. This usually creates a problem that you have to solve.

There are definite production support responsibilities and there will need to be employees assigned to each individual task or a group of interrelated tasks. They must communicate with each other, client management, finance, the shop foreman, the field foreman, and the quality control sections. (We'll talk more about quality control later on in this book.)

How frustrating is it when you deal with a contractor and his "project manager" is a twenty-five-year-old kid fresh out of college with a degree in construction management who has never been on a construction site? Sure, he knows every law in the book, he's taught a whole bunch of regulations and legal and safety stuff, but he couldn't tell you how big a 2" X 4" is. This is not a project manager. He may make a good assistant to the executive manager but he damn sure isn't going to correctly manage a project worth a crap. No one taught him how to do that.

I am not knocking these people. They have been trained in something, been assigned a position and duty, then placed on a jobsite to perform a job they really don't know about. The best trained people I have observed in the trades start at an entry level in a craft with a veteran tradesman as their partner to learn from and work their way up the ladder. This used to be called an apprenticeship. Remember those? You learned from the master and were paid to learn while you worked. Those need to be brought back to the industry.

The importance of having these sections correctly manned will make the difference between shop operations running smoothly or not; field projects running along smoothly or not; vehicles running or not; equipment operating or not. It is really that simple.

So now, let's have a look at what we have to know about the positions and duties of the employees that make up these sections so you can have an understanding of how this all works. Back in the day, these titles meant what they were intended to mean. Today they are thrown around as an expression of some kind of status symbol.

Have a look at the list below to get an overview of a **production support** team:

PRODUCTION SUPPORT MANAGER: The person responsible for the entirety of this section. It is their duty to see that the rest of the production support team get their jobs done without any kinks. He (or she) is the leader of the pack, with a thorough knowledge of the industry and its trades that your company is involved in. This person right here is one that started as a helper and worked their way up the ladder.

PROJECT MANAGER: This means exactly what it says; a person that manages one or more projects from start to finish. The project manager is responsible for providing all the support for a project, be it the materials, labor, supplies, vehicles, or equipment. This position is done from the office or in your facility and is the one who answers to all other positions regarding the project as well as the one that all other positions answer to. This person is not in the shop or on a jobsite, but would inspect it at regular intervals, and in addition, solve any kinks that come up for the projects under his/ her charge. This person deals with the client, architect and/or engineer, the shop manager, and the field operations manager to handle any discrepancies between what is on paper, what exists, and what must be produced as the final outcome. This position runs the project by schedule, handles documentation, and sorts out any discrepancies between what is real, envisioned, and required.

ASSISTANT PROJECT MANAGER: Assists the project manager in their duties on larger projects or when there are many projects to manage. This position can even manage smaller projects on their own under the watchful eye of a project manager.

PURCHASING AGENT: The person responsible for keeping the shop supplied with all its production supplies, materials, and rental equipment for projects; supplies for the office administration side of things; and booking travel and lodging arrangements. In a larger organization there will likely be several of these positions for different aspects of the company. This position answers for every single thing the company purchases.

LOGISTICS MANAGER: OK. So, what the hell is *logistics?* It is simply the movement of materials through the organization, coming in as raw materials and leaving as the finished product. This position is responsible for receiving the goods purchased and routing them to where they need to go. When the product is completed it is then this person's responsibility to ship it where it needs to go. Whether directly to a client-specified destination or to arrive on the jobsite, this person would make the arrangements and get it there cost effectively and on time.

SUB-CONTRACT MANAGER: This position has the responsibility of qualifying sub-contractors (subs) that are of the caliber to provide products and/or services to your company for the benefit of your clients and their projects. Once qualified as a sub for your company, this position handles and controls the schedule, documentation, legal requirements, payment applications, and delivery of products or services per the project schedule by the sub. This position makes sure that the sub provides what is required of them in the time frame it is required.

EQUIPMENT MANAGER: The equipment manager is responsible for the maintenance and repair of all the company's assets. This person develops and sees that scheduled maintenance for every vehicle, machine, or piece of equipment that the company owns is taken care of properly. He sees to it that any parts and maintenance supplies get purchased and plans scheduled shutdowns of production equipment for any needed repairs. This includes anything that must run or operate whether it's for production or facility operations such as plumbing, electrical, air conditioning, or heat. If it arises that something needs to be done by an outside vendor then this position handles that as well, coordinating with any other section in the company which it may affect.

EQUIPMENT TECHNICIAN: The person in this role is skilled in and performs the actions required on all the company-owned assets to keep them maintained and in perfect working order. There may be more than one of these, each with a special skillset. This position keeps everything maintained and repaired so that all the company equipment and facilities are usable, without any problems or interruptions in production or company operations.

While some production management teams might require additional personnel, these are the major players. They can be called by other titles to suit a specific industry.

Whether it's just a one-man show or two-hundred-employee company, somebody takes care of these positions and duties consistently or at one time or another. As the company grows from one to many, there will have to be employees that hold these positions exclusively. Without production support there will be little or no production and the facilities will be poorly maintained at best. Life will be miserable at work and there will be very bad morale. Your company will lose its best people because they will be unable to produce anything of value with pride and integrity.

As your company keeps going and growing you will exercise your ownership duties in recognizing, adding, and posting to this position roster, filling the duty positions as they arise.

Next, let's examine the **shop production** department. We are going to first cover the positions and duties as we did earlier. The list below outlines the positions and the duties for each of the prominent postings in this section.

SHOP MANAGER: The shop manager is responsible for the overall shop operations. This position guarantees the entire production area is operating at peak production, safely and without any unsolved issues. The duties include meeting with production support and field operations to provide the right products at the right time, every time. The shop manager solves any issues necessary to keep the shop performance at peak operating efficiency.

SHOP FOREMAN: In charge of the day-to-day production operations in the company's shop activities, the shop foreman makes sure quality products are being produced as per the timeline promised.

CREW FOREMAN: The person in charge of a crew that performs a group of tasks leading to a completed operation. There may be many of these crews consisting of a foreman and up to five or six production personnel, depending on the project size. This structure makes it possible to have the same small group execute a project from start to finish. Keeping the same personnel on the same project aides in completing the project without complications caused by frequently changing personnel.

TECHNICIAN: Any person skilled and experienced in mechanical or industrial techniques or in a particular technical field is titled "technician" and can be the plumber, electrician, welder, fitter, framer, or the like. The technician is sometimes called a tech or as a group, tech personnel. This position performs a specific function in the production sequence or they can be responsible for many functions of many projects, in the case of being part of a crew. The skills of these techs are the backbone of turning out high-quality craftmanship.

TECH ASSISTANT: The direct help person to assist the tech in their duties. Just like production support provides support for production, the tech assistant provides support for the tech. Whatever the tech's duty is, the tech assistant makes sure he or she is totally taken care of with tools, material movement, and supplies. The tech assistant performs duties and functions in the form of simple production tasks that support the tech.

MACHINE OPERATOR: The person who operates a production machine or piece of equipment that produces a piece of a finished product or a completed product. This could be a forklift driver, crane, drill press, metal brake, roller, or the operator of any other machine that does a function required to produce a specified end result.

Here we have the correct array of employees working to carry out all production demands of the company's clients, fulfilling each order perfectly, to specifications, on time and within budget, insuring adequate income for the company. Again, these can go by other titles to best suit the industry you are in.

Whatever it is that the company produces as a finished product or a component for a finished product, it is done by this group of employees. It may be that all these positions are held, and their duties performed, by just one person. In the case of a cabinet maker in his own shop for instance, the cabinet maker is responsible for all three sections as laid out in this chapter. He is also responsible for *every* position in his entire company! But he can only do so much.

One of the things I have experienced and seen others experience is that you may be able to do any of these duties as found in the organizing and running of a company. The difficulty begins when you need to perform *all* of these duties.

That is the exact reason that you need to fill in the chart with all of these positions, write a description of each position's duties, and as a result know exactly what has to happen in every phase of operation within the company. This way, you can clearly see how much each person does on a day-to-day basis. Then you can delegate to existing or newly hired employees.

In this last section we find the positions and duties of the **field operations** section. The following list lays out these positions.

FIELD OPERATIONS MANAGER: This position oversees all field work on every jobsite and responsibilities include correctly utilizing all the company resources available to guarantee the successful outcome of each and every field project. This includes making sure that the personnel in this section are of the necessary caliber required to execute the client's project perfectly as well as provide solutions to any problems that may arise. He or she makes sure that every base is covered and every requirement of the project meets or exceeds the client's specifications and expectations.

FIELD SUPERINTENDENT: The field superintendent position is boots on the ground, directly responsible for the work at a jobsite. Not only does this position have the duty of running the company's resources but it also has the duty of running any other subs required to complete the project. This is the person that makes it happen despite any odds and provides solutions to the real problems and kinks that are always a part of any project in the field. They are a solution-oriented person with the ability to overcome or reformat any barrier thrown at them and their personnel.

FIELD CREW FOREMAN: This person carries the same responsibilities as a crew foreman, with the exception that this person leads a crew on the jobsite.

TECHNICIAN, TECH ASSISTANT, AND MACHINE OPERATOR: These are the same positions and duties as listed earlier. The only exception is that these positions are skilled personnel in the duties required by the field environment on an actual client's jobsite.

There are different rules and regulations to follow on a jobsite that are not necessarily applicable in the shop. There may be certain background checks on all personnel. Most clients or general contractors have their own company policy concerning the requirements of being a contractor or sub-contractor on their jobsite.

A good field crew is a special breed of cat. These people are so competent as a group that they know what has to be done well enough that they can predict what each person in the group will do next. Their communication is done by observation of every action and hand signals.

These guys very rarely have to tell one another what has to happen next—they just recognize and do it. You'll know a good field crew when you see one. It is like watching poetry in motion. It is just action after action that is orchestrated in such a way that it appears absolutely effortless. Once you develop a crew like this, take care of them. They are worth their weight in gold.

Now that you have a basic understanding of the most important positions and duties of these sections, let's have a look at how they fit into your company.

If your company provides a finished product but no field operations, then you would only utilize the production support and shop production sections of this chapter. If your company only provides field operations, then you would only use the production support and field service sections of this chapter. If your company provides shop and field services then you would use all three sections: production support, shop production, and field operations.

Once this area of the company is laid out to review, then you begin to see how, without these production/delivery teams properly organized and running, the company will produce nothing, and no products or services can be exchanged for money, the fuel that propels the company through time. You can also see the importance of how the company works together as a whole and the interrelation with all the other sections thus far.

Partial staffing of these sections or staffing them with employees that are not completely capable of consistently performing the duties required can be the fastest way to ruin your company and its reputation.

Of course, the current size of your company will determine how these sections are complemented. You may have one person that holds several of these positions and performs their duties well and that may be the most ideal scenario.

The concept to pay attention to here is that you have a firm grasp of how the production and delivery area of the company works, how it's manned, and how it should perform. Then you can make the adjustments necessary to make it better than ever expected.

I have made the mistake of taking the best tech I had and promoting him to the shop foreman. Things started to go wrong, production lagged, and paperwork didn't get filled out. Morale suffered and the shop employees started talking garbage. When I asked the now shop foreman what was happening, he told me he didn't have any interest in the running of people and the administrative side of things. He was perfectly content being the best tech in the shop and that was his goal. So, that's what I returned him to. I promoted a different employee to shop foreman who had that goal and was capable of and interested in doing the best job possible. Everything went along perfectly.

The point of this is: know your employees well and utilize them in a win-win way, matching their goals and abilities to the best position and duties in the company.

Below are the key points of the production/delivery section of your company:

1. **PRODUCTION SUPPORT:** Does your company have the employees in place to fully support the providing of products and services to your clients? This section provides the personnel to make sure the production and delivery area of the company is completely supported in their activities. The employees in this section are there to back up

production and delivery of products and services to the client. They do nothing else but make sure that everyone and everything is available to the production and delivery personnel to properly and efficiently perform their duties. Production support does not do any of the actual work, they make it possible for the work to get done by the personnel whose responsibility it is.

Without this section the production area will not produce well because they will be too busy trying to manage and support themselves. There will be big gaps in production and employees will be pulling their hair out trying to do what should be—or already have been—done so they can do their duties.

How could this be? Just look at that ABC landscape company project we talked about in the last chapter. Without production support the field foreman would have ended up on the jobsite with no instructions, no personnel, no plants, no equipment and so, no production. It can't be stated any simpler, it's just that much of a no-brainer.

2. **SHOP PRODUCTION:** What does your shop production look like? Are there bottlenecks, areas where it always slows down or areas with the same problem over and over? Are there key personnel missing or not doing the job they should? Shop production is a primary income source for the company. Is the shop clean and organized? Is the flow through from raw material to finished product uninterrupted as well as without reversal? Reversal is the backward movement of something on the flow line of the shop. It means that something is traveling in the opposite direction it should. If it is not manned correctly it will look like an amusement park ride on the company's operating range graph that we learned about in the last chapter.

Let's talk a little bit about the flow through the shop from raw material to finished product. In any shop there are phases of production in different areas. Think of it as a roadway traveled from point A to point B. Raw material enters in at point A. Each individual production process should be performed in sequence, along the roadway, with the final finished product emerging at point B. Any movement backwards, over on to a side street, traffic jams, accidents, or construction on the roadway, costs time and money.

Every time someone handles a piece of material more times than it should be handled, it puts the project in danger of getting completed incorrectly or late. A process in the production might get skipped or measured from the wrong end for holes to be drilled. Sound familiar?

In the event that your company only provides shop production of some kind and not field operations, it is the *only* source of income for the company. If this section is not perfectly manned with the correct supervision and skilled technicians, then the company will never have an easy go of it. It will frequently be in trouble one way or another. There will be high turnover of employees and no one will be happy.

3. **FIELD OPERATIONS:** How well does your company perform on jobsites? Is the field superintendent getting results? Work in the field is fairly hard to control and run from a distance, unless of course you have someone who really knows his business on the jobsite and is taking ownership for it. Is the field crew a totally experienced bunch that you just marvel at for their accomplishments despite any and all odds? They should be.

    Keep in mind that if your company only provides field operations of some kind and not shop production, that will be the *only* source of income for the company.

    There are some interesting things that can occur with this set-up. You will be installing the products of a different company, which puts you at the mercy of the product manufacturer. What happens if the product is made wrong and you have to modify it to be correct? Without an excellent field crew and leadership, you'll go broke.

    It is ultimately a better scene to have a shop production section that makes the things that the field operations section uses or erects or installs. This gives the company an advantage to control both ends of the project, catching the mistakes or flaws before they happen.

Alright, I am done preaching to the choir. I trust you are to the point where you understand what's going on in these three sections. You might think I am looking over your shoulder because I know what you have been going through, but I'm not. I've seen these problems for over forty-six years in very many companies. And over just as many years they have not changed much—there are only bigger penalties for not knowing.

This is the main reason for writing this book. I want to help anyone in construction, trades, or any service industry to have the basic business operating knowledge and tools they need to fulfill their goals and dreams of having their own business.

So, let's get to filling out the chart for this chapter, which will help you see better how the current scene is within the company and how you could make it better. And remember, these titles are not carved in stone. You can make them the title that best fits your part of industry, but the responsibilities and duties remain the same.

EXERCISE 1: FILL IN THE THREE SECTIONS ON THE CHART FOR PRODUCTION SUPPORT, SHOP PRODUCTION, AND FIELD OPERATIONS AS THEY APPLY TO YOUR COMPANY

This will be a little different than you have been doing. This time you will put in the actual position titles in their respective sections from top to bottom in order as they appear in this chapter. If there are employees doing these functions put their names below the position title.

SUMMARY

As you can see, these three sections are really the income-producing arm of the company. All the other sections in the company cannot be there without these three and these three can't be there without all the others. Any company is one big giant team of individuals, each carrying a portion of the weight of a company.

If you are the only one in the company, my hat is off to you. Look what you are doing! It is quite a feat to perform all these duties.

If you are the leader of a section or even a whole company, you are applauded. To be able to lead men is no small ability. To lead them successfully as a team is a great skill.

We have all seen the word TEAM made into many different explanations of what it means, such as: **T**ogether **E**veryone **A**chieves **M**ore, but this doesn't factually describe what it means to be a real team. It only makes a statement about what a team could accomplish. Unfortunately, this is not always the case in real life. How many times have you seen a team where the weak ride the coattails of the strong?

There is a TEAM explanation which I have found to be all the way true and have written in my own words.

Technical experts at their duties

Each contributing specific strengths

All working uniformly together as one

Making a perfectly performing group

Using the principles and practices you are learning in this book, it is up to you to refine and apply them to your specific company and build that team.

Chapter Six

THE BASICS OF QUALITY CONTROL

Now it is time to look at the quality control section of the company. **Quality control** is the last line of defense to guarantee that the client receives exactly the products and services they order, preferably better than they expect.

Quality control, to most companies and in the mind of the employees, is making sure the product or service they provide has some level of quality. That it will be right. That it will not require any further work or correction. That the client is satisfied.

But it's way more than that. Quality control, QC for short, is a system for verifying and maintaining a desired level of quality in a product or service by careful planning, using proper equipment, ongoing inspections, and taking corrective action as required. Notice that it is a *system*.

That system, however, falls short of a complete QC section in almost every company I have seen. It falls short here—*and corrective action as required.* Most companies do fix the product or service before it gets delivered as a single end result, but there is no correction to the reason it happened in the first place. The cause of the problem is never corrected so it keeps on happening.

A funny example of this happened to me and one of my companies many years ago. We were on a high-profile government project fabricating and erecting a highly complex structural steel hangar. Every single weld had to be inspected by the client's welding inspector. We had about a dozen welders on site.

Every single weld always passed with flying colors, except those from one welder. He always flunked. When I checked this guy's welds myself, they were fine and I could not understand what was going on. This was costing us very precious time to redo work that there was really nothing wrong with.

So, I asked the welding inspector why he always flunked this one guy's welds. He said, "it's the human factor." What he was really saying was, "I don't like anything about the guy, therefore I am going to make everyone's life miserable until he gets straightened out."

Oh boy, how do I fix this? I talked to the inspector at length and the long and short of it is, he did not like the guy's attitude toward him or the way he talked to and treated his own team or other trades on the jobsite. The inspector figured if this guy was going to be a mean miserable bastard to everyone, then he would treat the guy just like the guy treated everyone else. The inspector was basically trying to make the guy's team responsible for getting him in line. I couldn't really fault the inspector because he was right—the guy was a mean miserable bastard. So, to control the quality of the project, I had to fix the guy.

So I had a long conversation with the welder. I got him to see that he was not treating others the way he would like to be treated. It was a humbling experience for him. He apologized to everyone for his behavior, even the welding inspector. After that, his attitude improved, he gained respect from each team member as well as the inspector, and he never flunked another weld inspection. And *that* is part of QC.

That welding inspector made me realize that "the human factor" is the principle reason you have quality or not. And so it goes, if there is a problem with quality, it boils down to a person. QC is responsible for seeing to it that not only the products and services get corrected, but also the people when those products and services suffer.

This could be the result of many things: the person doesn't know what their duties are; they are trying to do someone else's duties for which they are not trained; a change was made to the project and the techs were never told; the machine making the product was never fixed or maintained and therefore didn't work properly; and the beat goes on.

There are four key points for the QC section that we will review in this chapter. They are: product/service qualification, validation, training, and correction. Each of these are broken down further.

First we'll look at **product/service qualification.** *Qualification* is simply the verification of correctness, quality, condition, or required final result of any product or service. This is the inspection part of production. Is what is being produced exactly to specs, is the service being performed of the highest craftsmanship? Qualification is sometimes called *qual* for short.

If there are several steps to produce a component then there may be several steps to verify its correctness. In a project with many operations required, then there would be many points where a qualification inspection would occur. This is to make sure it is correct up until that point, then it can proceed to the next operation in the sequence.

As an example, when building a structure, or parts that make a structure, there are engineered drawings to follow. These plans tell one how to build each piece. As the pieces proceed through the shop, they should be checked at intervals along the way.

The most beneficial way to do the inspection is to compare each measurement in the process with what is on the project prints. Verify that everything about that piece is exactly what the print says it's supposed to be. If it passes, move it along.

Now, what if something doesn't pass? Well, you need to find out why and fix the problem. Who did it, or didn't, for that matter?

Your company needs its own inspectors to check the products and services being produced. In the shop it begins with the shop foreman. In the field it begins with the field superintendent. If they can't get the desired result then it gets reported to QC, who then steps in to find the root cause and correct the person or people responsible.

Some clients have their own inspectors, especially on larger projects. They camp out at your company or jobsite and inspect every aspect of everything you do or produce, at regular intervals in the process. This keeps you on your toes for sure!

In the shop and out in the field there has to be a direction to take to correct any mistakes. They are several ways you can do this. You can send the piece back to where it went wrong or have it corrected right where it is.

In any case use the best method that works for the company and the employees involved in it. Minimize delays in the correction process and make the corrections to the piece as economically possible and get production back to rolling at an optimum level.

You may find that there is an area of the shop or a specific field crew causing a never-ending stream of trouble. Look at the leader for the cause. When the leader messes up, it will be magnified all the way down the line.

No matter what your company's product or service is, you have to have a system in place to make sure the product being delivered or service being performed is exactly what was ordered. It's embarrassing when things are delivered and the next day you get a phone call that something is wrong with your work.

If the QC duties are performed correctly, verifying that the project was completed exactly to the engineering drawings and the product delivered still doesn't fit, then you did your job right and the engineer needs correction.

Make sure that each employee knows the importance of checking twice and doing the operation once. Make sure they know that nothing should be rushed, as that is just a sign of bad planning or scheduling and possibly the only real reason stupid mistakes in production occur. Remember, if there is not enough time to do it right in the first place, when will there be time to do it over?

Next we'll look at **validation**. *Validation* is simply an authority (in this case that of QC speaking for the whole company) declaring that some achievement has been reached or goal has been met and that it is official according to the statistics.

For instance, a lot of companies keep an "injury-free workdays" statistic. That is a validation of the company employees doing their job safely. And this is made into a game that all participate in, and if the injury-free workdays reaches 1,000 days then the company employees would be awarded a dinner banquet. This keeps the entire team responsible and accountable for each other's actions, which is very desirable as it keeps employees ethical.

Another example could be the "least number of products requiring correction per month." Of course you'd have to keep count every month. Let's say the number has been around thirty for several months for the number of products requiring correction before delivery. Well, make it a game to bring it down to twenty next month and all the employees involved get a pizza lunch if the goal is met.

I have found that we are really quick to jump on and crush the guy who makes the mistake that costs the company time and money. We should be just as quick to validate the guy that is an awesome crew foreman and perfectly completes his tasks all day, every day. This goes a long way in the success of the company as an action done by the QC department. A simple pat on the back and a "that-a-boy" is a validation, too.

And what about clients? Got any long-term clients? Ever award them with a plaque validating them for their loyalty? That's a different look at things, isn't it? Think of how much revenue your company has collected from a major client over a five-year period. How about spending a couple hundred bucks and presenting a plaque to them at their annual company dinner? This is unheard of in this day and age. Imagine the value of this QC action. *Wow.*

Add to the list suppliers and subcontractors. Your normal supplier always gets your order straight, on time. You never hear any complaints about your drywall sub. Validate them by giving them coffee mugs with your company's logo! This is no small thing, I assure you.

These are all quality control actions. Take these little steps and watch what happens. And yes, as you have undoubtedly realized, these are also promotion actions.

I'll tell you what will happen. You'll have people applying like crazy trying to become employees, more clients wanting your products or services, and suppliers and sub-contractors competing viciously to win your business.

The next key point is **training**. This is monumental in the QC scheme of things. Training covers some very specific orientation into the way your company operates.

More times than not, you hire an employee who is trained in their technical field. Be it a carpenter, bookkeeper, or machine operator, you hire the person because they have a proven track record and some sort of education or apprenticeship in their field. Some come with years of successful experience and some not so much.

So, naturally one would believe that if these people have been successful working for other companies, they will perform just as well in your company. This is a falsehood and is rarely true. (There are, of course, those that excel greatly no matter what company they work for and those gems are rare indeed.)

Chances are the new employee will come with a mindset developed by the policies of previous companies they have worked for, as well as the people they have worked with. The parameters are very different than those of your company yet the new employee will, unless trained in the policies and procedures of your company, use their previous ways of doing things. Nine times out of ten, those ways will not work with, fit into, or even be close to the policy and levels of standard of your company.

The new guy might be the best electrician on the block but he will not know about your company structure. How to requisition material, whether he should answer the phone or not, and whom to see or where to go when he has a problem.

That kick-ass electrician will be confused and develop a hatred for "management" simply because no one took the time to orient him into the organization, showing him where he fits in, why he is there, and the company policies he should follow. Then he'll start doing shoddy work followed by just never showing up for work, ever again.

The way to orient new employees is simple. Here is what HR does: Hires the person once he is cleared for employment. Gives him his position title, shows him where he is on the chart, and puts his name under the position he is holding. Brings him to finance to work out his payroll, taxes, any bank info, and gets that all squared around. Then brings him to the section of the company where he will work and introduces him to his supervisor.

The supervisor shows him to his workstation and introduces him to his teammates as applicable. Shows him where everything is, such as light switches, circuit breakers for the area, fire extinguishers, thermostat, bathroom, lunch station, first aid station, and any emergency or exit procedures. Shows him where he gets the supplies, materials and tools to perform his duties. The supervisor explains break and lunch times, start and end shift times, and any other important things regarding the new employee's position and duties.

You see, his basic training as he enters the company, no matter how informal it may seem, started the moment he (or she, of course) was hired. At this point, the employee is given your company's *Employee Handbook* and/or your *Company Policy Manual* and asked to read them and let the supervisor know when he has. It should be in short order, not weeks.

If your company has neither of these it would be a good idea to get working on them, especially since your company is going to experience rapid growth as you implement the concepts and ideas in this book.

Now the new hire goes to work. He gets grooved in and producing for one month. He gets to feel comfortable with the space, the supervisor and his teammates, and vice versa. If in a month there is not a benefit to the person, his teammates, and the company as a whole, it's not a good scenario—just let the new hire go. If he can't get it right in a month, he damn sure won't get it right in a year. Don't waste your time or money on any further training.

Let's say all involved fit nicely together and the new employee does well, is well liked, and brings benefit all around. The next step then is for the supervisor to bring him over to QC and introduce him to the QC manager. The QC manager does an interview with the person, not from an HR viewpoint, but to develop his skills and ability even more. This will enhance the quality control for the company and its products and services while improving the employee and his quality of life and work.

Here's an example: The person was hired as a forklift operator and he is damn good at it, keeping his area running timely, smoothly, and without incident. The person says he'd like to be a tractor trailer delivery driver for the company but does not have the commercial driver's license required. He says that years ago he learned how to drive a truck but had no reason to get his license so he didn't. There just happens to be an opening in the company for such a driver beginning on a part-time basis.

QC would get all the materials needed to study for the written test. The guy would study on his own time. The company would provide paid time to take the written test. When the guy passed, then QC would set up the road test and provide the truck and paid time off to take the road test. Now you have an employee who feels appreciated and will strive to do a perfect job at his duties, as well as be more interested in bettering himself and the company.

The above is just one of hundreds of possibilities. Make the employees more able and they make the company more able. This is what training is all about. It's a win-win relationship that can be exercised with all employees from the highest executive all the way down to the janitor in whatever area of technical expertise.

Through the years I have been fought heavily on this one concept as in the paragraph above. The usual argument is, that you get as much as you can out of every employee with as little given back as possible, lower wages included. "Because there are plenty more where they came from and if somebody doesn't agree with me let them quit or I'll fire them anyway."

I have also experienced the misfortune of working for some of these companies. They are horrible places to be, under a boss of such character. That is an example of what you don't want to create, as it is a suppressive environment where all lose—even the boss, eventually. You wouldn't want that to happen to you, so then why would you do it to others?

I have seen larger companies that have their own in-house course rooms where employees can take job skill courses, courses to manage their finances, improve their marriage, and a host of other training courses which simply make the person more able in all the steps of life. These companies are that big because of this. Wouldn't you want to work for a company like that? Wouldn't you want to build a company like that? Well, make no mistake about your abilities ... you *can* build a company like that.

The last key point of this chapter is **correction**. *Correction* is the making right of something which contains errors or faults. It is the removing of the flaws or errors found in the company's products, services, personnel, clients, suppliers, and sub-contractors. It is accomplished by finding the root cause of the error, fault, or flaw; correcting it (or them); and establishing a practice to keep the same thing from happening again.

Earlier in this chapter I mentioned that every problem could be traced back in some way to a person. This is a statement that is not easily agreed with by people sometimes. One of the greatest experiences I have ever had with this was not even in the workplace, but in my home. I, like most people, have a favorite coffee cup that I used every day. It was perfect.

One day I came home and my daughter approached me with a very frightened look on her face. I asked her what was wrong and she said, "Dad your coffee cup broke."

> I said, "Really, it was just sitting there next to the coffee pot and it just broke?"
> "Well, yeah," she said. "It just broke."
> I replied, "Did it run over to the edge and dive off and shatter to bits?"
> "Well no, it just broke."
> So I said, "Listen to what you are telling me. Was there an earthquake that knocked it off the counter?"

About this time she began to see that there was no way that it could just break by sitting there, no matter what she told me. She gave a big sigh of dismay and told me she knocked it off the counter by accident. I said, "Now that's more like it. Thank you for telling me the truth." And she asked me why I wasn't mad. I told her, "It's just a coffee cup; I can get another one." You see, the fear of penalty for breaking my favorite coffee cup was what led her to make up the "it did it by itself" story.

And the moral of the story here is this: **shit doesn't just happen**. It is made to happen by someone. Whether through direct action or taking no action at all, there is a person responsible for causing things to be good, bad, or indifferent.

One of the things you will run into is employees' fear of penalty when they make a mistake. This is usually born out of working for that less-than-desirable company and boss. They are used to working under constant penalty even if they do right. These employees are so scared of being fired that they run by the philosophy of hiding their mistakes with the attitude that QC will catch it before it goes out.

A person with that attitude will receive a penalty to fit the crime, as I am sure you agree. If that person doesn't correct the error of his/her ways then you have no choice but to let them go. There is intentional action to harm others and the company as a whole.

On the other hand, if the employee is loyal and honorable and will fess up to his or her mistake, then QC can get to the root of the problem and help them take steps to correct the cause by training, education, or in a way that helps the employee correct their own problem, whatever that may be.

Now what about this correction as it applies to clients? Ever had a client that once you made a contract they wanted to accelerate the schedule or change the design after you started production? Boy, do you have to educate them. Some clients require constant education in the process of production, and sometimes more than that on field projects. If you don't run QC on your clients they could easily bury the company.

I have dealt with clients that despite the QC section's best efforts, they just didn't get it and made the project a living hell, costing tons of money and missed schedules as well as late and shorted progress payments. When and if they come back requesting more service from the company, I'd just turn them away. It is just not worth doing work for these clients.

And how about suppliers and sub-contractors? Same thing. It is the constant observation of what these companies do with respect to servicing your company and your clients that tells the tale of whether they need correction.

If you experience late or substandard material deliveries or shoddy workmanship there is need for correction. You have to find out who was responsible and make sure the root cause is found and corrected so it does not keep happening and adversely affect your company—its products and services as well as its reputation.

A good company would see the error and agree to make it right and adopt a way to keep it from reoccurring. If they don't get that correction applied and continue to be substandard in any way, find a new more trustworthy supplier or sub-contractor. Again, to continue to do business with companies of this caliber will only bring heartache and grief, to say nothing of money and time thrown out the window.

Alright. Let's recap the key points of the QC section:

1. **PRODUCT/SERVICE QUALIFICATION:** What does your company do to ensure the product or service delivered to the client is flawless? This is the last line of defense to make sure the company only delivers products and services of the highest possible quality and correctness.

   Every company has to have a system for locating product flaws and errors or faults in service. Every employee in any company holds a level of responsibility in making sure quality products and services are produced by them and those around them.

   The amount of workload of this point of QC is directly determined by everyone in the production section. If all the production employees perform their duties correctly then it won't be much of a workload. More like a "business as usual" sort of thing.

QC does not stop at just getting the errors, flaws, or faults of the products or services fixed. QC goes all the way and gets to the root of why that thing is wrong and who did it and why they did it and gets correction applied all the way along the line.

2. **VALIDATION:** To let someone know they do a good job is a very important factor. It gives the person a sense of worth, a good attitude, and makes them strive to do a better job each and every day. Do you give credit where credit is due? Do you reward good production? Do you thank your clients for their business loyalty? Do you thank your suppliers and subs for watching out for your company as well as your clients?

All of this goes a very long way in developing the best employees and associates possible. It could be the difference between having smooth company operations with valued contribution to the expansion of the company or skating along with no real growth.

3. **TRAINING:** It is important that each employee is trained in the policies and procedures of the company structure and operation. It is the company's responsibility to make each and every employee be the best they can be. I know that is probably an overused cliché, but if you want people that excel at their duties, they must be trained at their position level on the chart, as well as being given the opportunity to advance in the company through training. It is the sad day when a bright tech assistant never gets the opportunity to become a tech within the walls of the company.

Does the company offer training? It should as this is how you build and expand a company through the value of its employees, as well as improve their lives.

Does your personnel keep your clients in check through educating them? Do your suppliers and subs have a good grasp on the company's products and services so they can provide your company, and your clients, the best possible support?

As you can see, training has many places in the company, done naturally by good leaders and responsible employees. It is QC that gets involved when normal instruction doesn't improve the condition and threatens the company's products/services or otherwise puts the company, its projects, or employees at risk.

4. **CORRECTION:** Usually a manufacturing company does a spot inspection on their products, taking maybe 1 item in every 100 to inspect. That may be OK when a production run of a product is 10,000.

In the construction industry damn near every action performed requires inspection. This is evident just by reading the list of inspections required to build something as published by your local building department. Is it not true that every sub has QC on their own work, making sure it is correct, so it passes the code requirements? In other words, the quality required is stated in the building codes of what each contractor or sub-contractor must provide as a level of craftsmanship for their trade. So a form of QC is already being provided that personnel must meet whether their company has a QC section or not.

Again, we can see that QC is performed to some extent by every employee in every section of the company. It is QC that once again gets involved when the normal course of operation does not solve the issue. If one guy just keeps messing up despite the efforts of the shop supervisor, then the supervisor sends him to QC to get straightened out.

QC, as an important part of its duties, corrects the person who has some kind of a "blockage" preventing him or her from performing their duties. While HR handles the administrative side of each employee, their placement and interrelations with the company and its personnel as a whole, QC locates the reasons for and helps correct any abnormal situations with the individual person.

The same holds true for your clients, suppliers and subs; if they don't see the light as shined by the normal actions from the respective sections of the company, sic QC on them to get to the root of the problem and correct it.

Alright. It is time to fill in the chart again.

EXERCISE: FILL IN THE QUALITY CONTROL SECTION ON THE CHART

Go to the chart you are making and list out the four key points of quality control in the column under "Quality Manager." Just like you have been doing, leave space between them. Then under each key point list out the position held and its duties as they relate to your organization, no matter who does them. If there are people doing them besides you, put their name there.

SUMMARY

You may find that there is no QC system or the functions are being performed by very few alert people in the company. Or maybe it's only done on an emergency basis where a crew has to be kept all weekend to correct what has to go out on Monday morning.

Chances are you will have your best crew do this. They didn't make the original mistakes in the first place, yet they're the ones now being penalized to work the weekend.

Oh yes, this is the fault of the shop manager not being responsible for his part of producing quality products. You better find out what's going on and correct his ass, but quick.

Now you can see that QC is a bit more involved than most people think and that most companies fall far short in their QC actions. A complete QC section is critical as it brings incredible value and quality to your products, services, and to your organization as a whole. This chapter has given you have the tools to build a QC system that works 100 percent of the time.

Quality control is not just about making sure the finished product delivered or services performed are what they are supposed to be, but also finding the root of the problem and putting in corrective actions so errors, flaws, and faults are not made. Correct the person and you fix the problems.

Quality control is done, to some degree, by everyone in the company as applicable to their position and section. It is that level of responsibility to the company as well as every other team player in it that determines the success of the company and the individual's lives that make the company.

Be sure to assign people skilled in the activities of QC as it relates to the products and services of your company and make sure they are following these principle and procedures.

If all the employees have pride, integrity, and responsibility for their position and duty in their day-to-day conduct, QC is the least busy of all the sections.

Chapter Seven

THE BASICS OF CREATING NEW BUSINESS

N ew business is way more than just new customers, it is public relations that put the company on the map. So let's get started on breaking this into understandable key points. They will be *direct advertising for new business, new business through referrals,* and *community involvement.*

First, let's discuss **direct advertising for new business.** This is how your company gets new clients and further expands the company to keep it going and growing. Without doing this, your company will not grow and over time will eventually begin to shrink.

Why? Because if you don't get new clients, in excess, to replace those that fall off or go under, your company will have less work and will struggle to keep going and stop growing. This is just inevitable. And the bigger the company becomes the more it will require to keep going and growing. Plainly put, the bigger the machine, the more it costs to fuel it.

Again, I would like to make sure that you remember, this is done on the company's proven basis within its successful operating zone as covered in Chapter Four. Never violate that operating zone of the company beyond its ability to successfully deliver and recover. You push that operating zone only to the degree that you end up back in it higher than you were before you pushed it.

As discussed in Chapter Three, advertising is the actual message (promotion) targeted and delivered to the consumers of particular goods or services (marketing) through any medium. A *medium* is the place you put your promotion, be it a newspaper, mailing, internet campaign, etc. The important thing to know is that you have to create good promotional material and deliver it to your targeted market.

So, what is a targeted market? Prospective clients that readily use the products and services that your company provides to support their operations.

If you're like me and you go to the gun range, you shoot your bullets to hit a target. This is the same concept as reaching your target market. Look at the gun as the medium, the bullet as the promotion, and the target as the correct audience receiving the promotion.

Let's say that you have a concrete contracting company. The major services provided are to form and pour concrete slabs, produce concrete block walls, and do brick work. You would not advertise for new business in a plumbing contractor magazine. You shot the bullet way out in left field somewhere, not even coming close to the target. That would be an incorrect target for new business, to say nothing of wasted advertising dollars.

So, where would that concrete contracting company spend their advertising dollars to create incoming requests from prospective new clients? One way is to simply look at the types of companies you've been working for. As a concrete contractor, you find that your company has done the majority of its work for general contractors that build new homes or commercial buildings.

Great! That is your target market. General contractors. OK, what do you do now? The first thing is to develop a promotional piece that will appeal to any prospective client. It'll show who the company is, how long you've been in business, projects done, testimonials, and contact info. It could include any other info that may be vital to them getting to know your company as well as the products and services it provides.

Don't clutter it up. Clutter is the reason why you throw away all the promotion you get now, whether it has anything to do with you or your company or not. The first and biggest words and colors are what determines if the person will have their interest sparked enough to read the rest of the promo. If the prospect has to make an effort to make sense of the thing, it goes in the trash. If the style of letters is really cool, but almost impossible to read as some are, it's going in the trash.

Always try to address your promo to a person or position in the company you're sending to. If you send it to "Occupant at" or "Our friends at," it's going in the trash.

Make sure your contact info brings the prospective client to a specific person holding the position in your company who is schooled in the proper communication, introducing that prospective client to your company, so the client is handled professionally, courteously, and swiftly.

There is nothing more aggravating than calling a company because you need something they produce, then getting bounced all over the phone, ending up finally at the last person only to leave a voicemail. You rightfully feel like you have gotten nowhere. And you still don't know where to go, but you sure want to tell them where to go.

There are several mediums to put your promotion out on. It could be a flyer, postcard, or even an e-mail campaign. It could be an ad in the local newspaper, but let's face it, who reads a newspaper anymore?

You could attend some of those network lunches that people always talk about. These networking groups pop up, are around for a while, then they disappear and a new one pops up in its place. I remember going to these types of networking meetings about fifteen years ago. The food was pretty good but I only stayed just to figure out what all those people were doing. I never got any business from them. Hah! Wrong market!

Making phone calls where you would follow up to interested parties by sending them a brochure is also a possibility for promoting your company. You might also do a walk-in and deliver the promo personally.

To do phone calls and walk-ins, for me, is still the best form of not only getting to know your target market, but also, it lets those people know that there is substance to your company. Sort of proves that there is a company there. It gives them an actual person they can call that they have met, or at least talked to on the phone, so they know there is someone real there.

Mailed postcards and flyers are probably the next best, especially if they get treated right when the receiver reaches out to your company. That first contact will determine if they continue to develop a relationship with the company or not.

E-mail campaigns work, but for me, and my experience with them, the amount of e-mails that have to be sent out for any acceptable rate of return is astronomical. Also, by law, you need to meet certain criteria when doing e-mail campaigns, as laid out in the CAN-SPAM act of 2003, which regulates the way you lawfully send commercial e-mails. There are those that are successful with it, and it is worth testing.

Call me old school, but I still believe in face-to-face communication. It has also been the most successful medium to promote with that I have used to date. Postcards, flyers, e-mails can go out in quantity, inexpensively. It is very important to follow up on those actions, in person or on the phone, and this is where the negotiating happens and the deal gets made.

Another thing your company needs is a kick-ass website. In this day and age, especially if there is no face-to-face, your company *must* have an online presence. It is a first point of entry to your company. It has to perfectly represent your company to the prospective client. It is the medium on which that prospect will determine whether or not they even want to contact you to do business. The company's website needs to be a true representation of your organization with several ways to contact your company.

An additional avenue for advertising is giving seminars promoting the company. This is where you would invite an audience of prospective clients to a space at your facility and give them the lowdown on your company, its products, services, a review of successful projects, and an overview of how your company is the best choice to support their operations. It should be about an hour or so long and include a tour of the company facilities if given in-house. They should leave with your brochure in their hand.

Advertising in trade publications is another option. Keep in mind though that these are pretty much reserved for larger companies. It cost a pretty penny to get a noticeable ad in these due to the fact that the prospective clients do projects in the tens and even hundreds of millions of dollars. When your company can efficiently provide a single project yielding an income of three million or above, then you would consider placing ads in a trade publication.

If the company did a million annually it would probably be too small to advertise in a trade publication. The projects to bid on in this medium would most likely be in excess of what the company is able to perform with its current resources.

Now, there is nothing wrong with getting to know who those larger companies are and the size of projects they perform or establishing a relationship with them for the future. As in any industry, there is a broad but tight network where people talk, so getting in the door at any level is good. It is a way to get other prospective clients to look at your company now.

Trade shows are also a very good way to advertise. It takes a bit of vision and work to make a positive impact on those at a trade show. A couple of people sitting at a folding table won't do it. You'll have to a have a very professional presentation with several employees manning the area that know the company well and can provide the right answers to any questions. You'll want to have giveaways like coffee mugs, pens, notepads, maybe even brochures. Something that keeps your company name in their sights for the next long time.

Trade shows can be expensive, which is why they need to be done right. But, and that is a capital BUT, just one client made from a trade show can easily pay for its expense.

The excellent thing about a trade show is that clients of every size and scope go to them. It is a venue where you can *really* get the word out on your company very broadly. You can even pick trade shows that target the right market for your industry.

Another benefit is there are usually conferences where new developments and technology is taught, which shows your people new resources to modernize and economize on the company's best practices. I have even seen apps and other tablet-based tools released at trade shows that make jobsite duties way easier. If you have never been to one, you should pick one out for your industry and go as an observer. You'll have a blast.

Now let's move on to covering **new business through referral.** A referral is just what it sounds like. It is when someone *refers* your company (or you) to someone else as a resource. They recommend your company's products and/ or services to others that are looking for a provider of them.

If you have an excellent reputation this will occur naturally. I have even seen someone refer a company to one of their associates just because the promo they saw on the company impressed them, without them ever having used the company themselves. This is the power of good advertising.

There are suppliers that can refer clients to your company. Often, suppliers get calls from clients searching for something they do not directly provide. The supplier will naturally recommend the first capable resource that comes to mind. If your company has good standing relations with the supplier, that will be you.

The sub-contractors you use are another voice for your company. Provided your company has good relations with them, those people will naturally recommend you to a client searching for what your company does.

This is why it is so important to maintain good relations with everyone your company does business with or associates with. As we have already learned, these are all promotional activities that feed the ideas to people of what you are all about.

My grandfather used to say "If you satisfy your customers you'll always have them—if you don't, they'll make sure you have none." This is true from every angle, whether clients or any other business the company has a relationship with. And so it is with the broad but tight network in the construction industry. You have undoubtedly experienced this industry, and the pitfalls it creates if a company delivers badly on just one project. Bad press spreads fast.

To carry on, there are even companies that broker services to prospective clients. You know them, you just don't realize that's what's going on there. How about Angie's List, HomeAdvisor, or Houzz? These are referral companies, short and sweet.

A larger company would probably recommend your company to a smaller one. I have seen this happen. A huge company that knew of a contractor that was too small to provide services for them recommended that contractor to a client that did smaller projects. This was the beginning of a longstanding relationship that lasted many years.

Once the contractor became big enough to effectively deliver those bigger jobs, the larger company remembered and respected that contractor for what it had accomplished thus far. Then a new relationship was established with the larger company.

This is all what is called word-of-mouth advertising. It comes about as a direct result of your reputation in the industry, the extent that you are looked at as an industry leader, the general appearance of your facilities and workforce, the state of your vehicles and equipment, even how clean you keep your premises and jobsite activities. All of these, and more, contribute to the image projected into the eyes and ears of any prospective new client.

Make no mistake, this is a very powerful influence in the ability of your company to attract new business. If your company's reputation is mud, you'll definitely be in it!

Another interesting and effective way to develop new business is pay a commission to individuals for bringing in a new client that enters into a contract with your company. You can set up an entire network of sales people without ever having them on your payroll. This would be your sales representative network. They would be divided into their own geographical service area. They would be educated about your company and the employees in it and supplied with the promo material necessary to make the best presentation with the sole purpose of sending the prospective client to your company. The sales rep would be paid a commission on any contracts received as a direct result of his or her efforts.

This is an effective way to expand your company to perform in a larger service area without any real costs. In companies that have multiple locations, this is, undoubtedly, how they started in a different area. The sales rep creates the demand, the company performs the service, and this is repeated. This goes on until the company's reputation in that area is developed so well that the company establishes a branch there.

In a smaller company that is expanding, this is a good way to develop new business. By using a sales rep network, you don't need to have many full-time sales people on the payroll. You will need one good manager to oversee many outside sales reps and help them get their job done, as well as handle those prospective new clients correctly, turning them into long-term clients of the company.

Lastly in this chapter is **community involvement.** It is important to recognize and take care of the community where your company is located as well as where you live. This is often called "giving back." It is far more than that, though.

It is taking responsibility for the people and environment that fall into your area of influence. It is making sure that these people and places are helped and maintained in general. It is volunteering for the activities that strengthen the community, improving its appearance, removing of dangers in the environment, or providing help in emergency situations. It is helping your local church and associate businesses in desperate times. It is doing whatever you can to make the environment safe, beautiful, and desirable.

There are some very cool ways a company can accomplish this and gain recognition for their contributions. Sponsor a Boy or Girl Scout troop, Little League team, or school sports program. Imagine seeing your company name right under "sponsored by" on the team uniform. If that doesn't make one proud, I don't know what does.

Many of the sports activities in schools are going away due to budget cuts. It's the time to step up to the plate and give children the same opportunities we had as kids. We should not allow changing times to strip our youth of activity or opportunity. Today's youth are tomorrow's leaders. Don't lose sight of that. Do what you can to help.

Understand here that your company could provide a volunteer work force for community clean-ups, neighborhood watch, or just bringing ole' lady Higgins her groceries once a week. If your church puts on holiday events, then provide volunteers as well as a donation to cover some of the needed supplies.

We have all heard of contractors that "rebuilt Harriette's house after the fire" or some such thing. This is taking responsibility for the community. You will personally feel and be more alive and content because of it. Don't think so? Go ahead and give it an honest try.

Whatever you, your company, and your employees can do to improve the environment and help others, at a level that it can afford, will come back in your direction ten-fold. The concept here is help where you can, when you can, and at the capacity you can.

This is all a form of public relations. Public relations is really just how you conduct your company's affairs in and with the public sector, and as a result of those actions, how the public sees and relates to you. If you and your company do favorable things, then the public will view those things favorably and probably make those actions a topic of favorable conversation. You do unfavorable things or no things at all, well, then … you get the idea.

Although community involvement will gain you good press for your contributions, this is not the real reason why you should do it. You do this because if don't, then chances are no one will. If you lead in taking responsibility for the community, then your company becomes an example, causing other people, companies, and organizations to pitch in and do the same. Through the efforts of all contributing, the community becomes a shining example of where most people want to live. It keeps going and growing.

This is how you build the world you want around you, the world you want to live in, the world others want to move to and participate in, while at the same time building your company and its own people, as well as other companies and organizations. As a united and powerful force we can build a better world in which to live.

OK. Let's recap the key points of getting new business:

1. **DIRECT ADVERTISING FOR NEW BUSINESS:** Your company needs some really awesome promo material aimed at new clients as well as a dazzling website, helping to establish an online presence. There has to be a targeted market to promote to that is economical and brings results in the form of new clients jumping on board with your company. And you will also need to delegate the activities for new business advertising as well as set up employees that know how to take care of new clients at the point of entry and send them along the right roadway into and through your company.

    The goal here is to attract new clients through successful advertising programs and establish them as loyal, repeat clients.

    As you have already figured out, there must also be sufficient company resources to service each new client properly. You have to be a pretty keen manager to make it all happen for prosperity rather than doom.

2. **NEW BUSINESS THROUGH REFERRAL:** Your company needs a manager (employee) and a sales rep team (commission-based outside sales). The goal here is to attract new clients through successful personal contact and promotion as well as with advertising programs to establish prospective clients as loyal, repeat clients. This is done by specific geographic location even if in your own established area.

3. **COMMUNITY INVOLVEMENT:** Your company should have policy established that encourages employees to volunteer and contribute to community activities and social betterment projects. Make it your goal to lead the way, setting the example by helping to improve your community and creating the kind of place that you want to live in and where others will contribute by helping to create a safe, stable environment for all. One where all folks can do well and enjoy a happy, healthy lifestyle.

And now it's that time again to return to your chart.

SUMMARY

Again, it is important to point out that while it initially may seem like more work is being created, implementing the systems and tools suggested here will help your business grow and flourish. Keep in mind that you are building a company structure where other employees can hold these positions, fulfill these responsibilities, and perform these duties so you don't have to. It is your duty to empower your employees with this book and allow them to create the company just as you would.

Gaining new business is an essential ingredient to keep your company going and growing. It includes several strategies and activities, not just "How can I get new business?"

You see, a company is only as good as the people that work it and take responsibility for it. Others notice these things. If a company rapes the environment and reduces its employees to robotic morons, people notice. If a company skates along and never really amounts to anything, people notice. People talk. People spread bad news very carelessly.

A company that represents itself truthfully, provides stellar products and services time and again, and takes part in creating a better world around them, people really notice. They will spread that news carefully. They will help and get others to help create that better world. No one dreams about going downward, most people dream about going upward.

Help make it so.

THE BASICS OF OPERATION

I n this last chapter we are going to have a look at how to tie it all together and what methods are used to make it all flow through the company.

While there will be a fair amount of brilliance and work required to set up the system, once in use, you'll be able to catch and correct any problems, even before they become problems. It will be so easy to watch the flow of a project through the company, you won't believe it.

Before I get into this, I want to cover four positions on the chart we have not yet reviewed. These positions are in the four boxes right below the top box, "Owner," and preside over one or more sections. They are:

EXECUTIVE MANAGER – Responsible for the overall company. This position has the duty of making sure the company goes and grows through his/her knowledge of business, the industry, and good planning and management. This person has the ability and care to keep every section of the company running like clockwork.

ADMINISTRATIVE MANAGER – Directly responsible for the administration, client management, and finance sections of the company. This position takes care of running these three sections and makes sure they do the duties without error and in conjunction with all other areas of the company.

OPERATIONS MANAGER – Directly responsible for the production/delivery and quality control sections of the company. It is their duty to make sure that these areas operate smoothly, without incident, and solve any problems swiftly and to a definite final result.

PUBLIC RELATIONS MANAGER – Directly responsible for the new business section of the company. It is this position's duty to create programs which make a steady stream of new business come into the company for products and services, as well as put the company on the map as a leader in its industry and community.

These four positions are above all others on the chart, excepting of course the owner, for good reason. They are the gods in their fields with exemplary skills and abilities, working together to keep the company going and growing. These are positions of extreme trust.

These are the positions that guarantee your exit plan. When these positions take care of business, you are free to go on vacation whenever you want, with no worries.

You can back out of the company, monitor it from afar, collect an income, and even venture off into other areas of interest.

In a newer or smaller company these positions may not be filled or you may have a tough time finding the right person to fill one. Don't lose any sleep over this. As you add employees to meet growth demands, keep your eyes on everyone you hire for the purpose of finding the right people to train and fill these positions.

OK. So, to the operation of the company. How are we going to tie all this together and make it flow like a well-bordered river?

Each project is run step-by-step as an executable program[1] written in the form of a checklist. Each project is programmed from start to finish and kept track of on the checklist. Each section manager is responsible for keeping track of the progress of the project, including all the paperwork and documentation required, as well as monitoring and correcting any delays, problems, or kinks experienced.

So what is a **checklist?** A checklist[2] is a written form with a list of steps and/or actions that when performed in the proper sequence produce a specific end result. It could be used for many different reasons, including inspection, confirmation of work performed, or routing a project through the company.

A checklist can also be called a *routing form*.[3] It is easy to see why, because as you do the steps, it routes the project through the company lines and positions from start to finish.

Similarly, a checklist can be written to put a project, or even an employee, on the starting line into your company and programmed on the right road to proceed through it in an organized manner.

Any of these checklists are proprietary to the companies that have them. Each checklist is written with the company, its products, services, and positions as the determining factor. It makes the person or thing follow a prescribed path to an end result.

You can certainly, with some imagination, follow a process from beginning to end and come up with a checklist to program it for all its steps, all its points where it needs to be, the actions required at those points, all the way through to the final finished product.

Checklists can take many forms. The important idea to follow is that each step along the way requires an employee to perform a specific operation. This gives each employee the knowledge of where the person or project stands in relation to what has been done and what needs to be done.

For example, a technician can use a particular checklist to check over a piece of equipment to make the equipment ready for or keep it in service. We have seen these in day-to-day operations. The tech inspects the forklift with a checklist on a regular basis to verify all systems are ready to go. Below is an example daily checklist for a forklift.

FORKLIFT OPERATOR'S DAILY CHECKLIST
(Complete Before the Start of Each Shift)

Date:	Truck #:	Location:	Shift:
☐ Engine	☐ Electric	Hour Meter Reading:	
Operator:		Technician:	

CHECK ANY DEFECTIVE ITEM WITH AN X AND GIVE DETAILS BELOW.

	ACCELERATOR		HOUR METER
	ALARMS		HYDRAULIC CONTROLS
	BATTERY CONNECTORS		LIGHTS - HEAD TO TAIL
	BATTERY FILL LEVEL		LIGHTS - WARNING
	BELTS		MAST
	BRAKES - PARKING		OIL LEAKS
	BRAKES - SERVICE		OIL PRESSURE
	CABLES		OVERHEAD GUARD
	ENGINE OIL LEVEL		RADIATOR LEVEL
	FORKS		SAFETY EQUIPMENT
	FUEL LEVEL		STEERING
	GAUGES		TIRES
	HORN		UNUSUAL NOISES
	HOSES		OTHER _____

DETAILS: _____
_____
_____
_____
_____
_____
_____
_____
_____

MAINTENANCE COPY

As you can see, this is a visual inspection that the forklift driver does daily. He would write down any problem he found where it says DETAILS. Notice that this says MAINTENANCE COPY. This copy would be sent to the tech responsible for equipment maintenance and repair in the production support team. The tech would then check out the forklift and fix anything the driver found wrong. The original would be kept by the driver.

Although you should have a checklist like this for every piece of equipment the company owns, it may not have to be done daily. Depending on the kind of equipment, it could require a weekly, monthly, or even an annual checklist for inspections, operations, or maintenance required. Almost every piece of equipment you buy will have the required checklists in the owner's or operator's manual. Make copies of them and use them.

This is how you keep track of all the company equipment, its service, and repairs. A copy of the completed checklist should go into the equipment's file so there is a running record of every action ever performed. This is also a tool to find out if the employee assigned to perform those duties is doing their job.

A checklist can also be used to put a new employee in position. Below is a checklist that a new employee follows to make sure all the required steps are done to get him or her properly initiated into the company. This is a very basic checklist and will probably need modification for your particular company's use.

NEW EMPLOYEE CHECKLIST

Purpose of this checklist: To get the new employee through all actions necessary to be properly signed on as an employee and to become familiar with the company and how it operates.

The HR manager or their assigned employee is to start this checklist with the new employee. Have him/her read the purpose of this checklist and make sure they have a general idea of what it is for. Answer any questions they might have but get them started on the checklist because doing the form will answer the majority of their questions. Have them check off the actions as they do them to keep track of what has been done.

☐ HR manager: Give the person a New Employee Packet with all the necessary forms.

Employee Name: _____

Date: _____

☐ 1. Fill out each of the following forms in the packet you have been given. If you have any questions about any of the forms, you can ask the person who gave you the packet.

- EMPLOYEE WITHHOLDING FORM (W-4)
- EMPLOYMENT ELIGIBILITY VERIFICATION FORM (I-9)
- MODEL RELEASE FORM
- EMERGENCY CONTACT INFORMATION FORM
- NEW HIRE AGREEMENT

☐ 2. Once the forms are complete, turn them in to the HR manager, who will make a personnel file. This file will be a permanent record of your employment with the company.

☐ 3. Ask the HR manager to make a copy of your driver's license.

☐ 4. Go into the reception area and ask the receptionist for an Orientation Checklist and complete it.

☐ 5. Once you have completed the Orientation Checklist, give it to the HR manager so it can be put in your personnel file.

☐ 6. Get a copy of the Employee Handbook and read the first nine pages.

☐ 7. Go to your assigned section and introduce yourself to the section supervisor.

☐ 8. Get an overview of your duties from your section supervisor and visit your new workstation.

☐ 9. Return this completed checklist to HR, who will verifiy it's done and put it in your personnel file.

END OF CHECKLIST

As you can see, the new employee follows this checklist along with company personnel of the various sections. This way, all that needs to be known and done follows through with the applicable company personnel who are responsible to make sure that all paperwork is done correctly and completely.

When doing a job in the shop, it is necessary to track a project through administration and production at the same time. I have put together example checklists for this in this chapter. If you have never done this before, you may find reading the checklists a little confusing.

Use these as examples and make ones that fit your company operations. Then print them out and run yourself along the path through the company. Keep working them and changing them until they work flawlessly in tracking every movement and step along the way from start to finish through the company. Each checklist must hit every necessary step at every necessary point in the operation to guarantee that the desired end result is attained for the project.

Once you do this, then every project (or operation) can be done with the same checklists, folder arrangements, and steps, bringing each one to a successful completion. A checklist should be designed so it is relatively easy to follow, making it possible for any employee to use it regardless if they have ever used one or not.

First we will look at the administrative (office) checklist for a project.

PROJECT CHECKLIST - OFFICE FOLDER

Purpose: To get all pertinent data into the folder and into the hands of the appropriate employees rapidly so there are no slowdowns or stops on the administration lines.

CLIENT NAME:		Client P.O. #:	
		Client Job #:	
Billing Address:		Client Contr. #:	
JOB NAME:			
JOB NUMBER:		Submittals:	
JOB ADDRESS:		Workers Comp. Ins./ Gen'l Liability	
Brief Job Description:		Certifications	
T&M Shop Field Crane		Business Licenses	
Contacts/Phone #s:		Certifications	
		Auto Ins. Certs.	
Terms: (Circle One) Adv. Pmt. COD Net 30 Contract		Certified Payroll	

Total Contract Amt:		Application for Pymt.	
Start Date:	Completion Date:	Partial Lien Release	
Payment Terms:		Sub/Con. Warrantee	
		Final Release of Lien	
Billing should be received by:_____		Scope of Wk. Docs.	

EXECUTIVE MANAGER

☐ 1. Verify correctness of the contract.

☐ 2. Make an office folder for the project.

☐ 3. Fill in all data at the top of this form.

☐ 4. Put the job name on the tab of a manila file folder to be used in the office.

☐ 5. Put the contract documents and any other administrative notes in the office folder.

☐ 6. Send the office folder to finance manager.

☐ 7. Start a production checklist and make a green production folder. Place all the plans, drawings, specifications, schedule, and all documentation required for production into the folder. Send the production folder to the sales manager.

FINANCE MANAGER

☐ 7. Log job data into computer (name, address, job #, etc.)

☐ 8. If possible, create an invoice in the accounting program which shows correctly any money collected, what is to be billed and amounts due. If not possible now, do it as soon as you can.

☐ 9. See that all **submittals** marked on the top of this page are sent immediately.

☐ 10. Get a copy of your customer's annual resale certificate if you are not charging them sales tax. Put the copy in the annual resale certificate folder.

☐ 11. Send the office folder to the sales manager.

SALES MANAGER

☐ 12. Check over all the information in the office folder and make sure it is correct and complete. If not make any corrections required in red ink and get any required documentation to make it complete.

☐ 13. Send the office folder to the finance manager.

☐ 14. Check over the production folder information and make sure it is all correct and complete. If not, make any corrections required in red ink and get any required documentation to make it complete.

☐ 15. Send the production folder to the operations manager.

FINANCE MANAGER

☐ 16. When the deposit is collected, notify the operations manager in writing of the amount received.

☐ 17. Put folder in the "in progress" bin until you get the production folder back as complete. Always check for any billing that can be done before the twenty-fifth of each month so the payment can be received by next month.

☐ 18. When you receive the production folder back, begin to close out the project.

☐ 19. Verify that the Statement of Completion has been signed. (production checklist item #25)

☐ 20. Create an invoice now if one was not already done.

☐ 21. Complete any submittals needed to get final payment. Example: certified payroll, G702, G703, lien release, etc.

☐ 22. Bill for any unpaid balances and/or retainage sums.

☐ 23. Note status of balance due at this time:

☐ 24. Log data into collections sheet.

☐ 25. File folder in collections bin and call client when balance is due.

☐ 26. Collect balance, reconcile job account, and if the correct amount has been paid, deposit the check into our account. (Make copies of the check and put it into the folder.) If the wrong amount has been paid, find out why and get the right amount paid.

☐ 27. Notify the operations manager that the final balance has been collected on this job.

END OF CHECKLIST. LEAVE IN THE FOLDER ONCE COMPLETED.

The above checklist tracks the project through all the administrative actions required on a construction project. Again, this is just an example. It may work for your company or it may be partially or totally off base. The purpose is to help you understand the importance of them so that every single step in every single operation can be accomplished, producing the desired end result.

OK. Here is the companion production checklist for a project.

PROJECT CHECKLIST - PRODUCTION FOLDER

Purpose: To get all necessary information into the hands of production rapidly so the product or service contracted can be produced exactly as ordered and delivered as quickly as possible.

CLIENT NAME:			
JOB NAME:			
JOB NUMBER:			
Job Site Address:			
Brief Job Description:			
Contacts/Phone Numbers:			
Project Manager:			
Field Superintendent:			
Resident/Owner:			
Start Date:	Be on the site at:	:	AM PM
Completion Date:			

OPERATIONS MANAGER

☐ 1. Make sure everything required is in the production folder.

☐ 2 Meet with production support and the shop/field manager to kick off the project.

☐ 3. Make the schedule for the project that meets or exceeds the client's requirements.

PRODUCTION SUPPORT

☐ 4. If required, get the field measurements and fill in the **Required Tools Checklist**.

☐ 5. Get shop drawings ordered as soon as possible.

☐ 6. Keep in touch with detailer and get drawings approved quickly.

☐ 7. Check existing stock and the get needed material lists made if not already and get at least three quotes on material.

☐ 8. Get material ordered from the supplier that will deliver on time for the best price.

☐ 9. Delivery date:_____(**Note**: Date should be one week ahead of start date in shop)

☐ 10. Put all required checklists into folders (safety, field survey, etc.)

☐ 11. Put Sign-Off/Completion form into the folder if needed. Circle item #25 below.

☐ 12. Note where the plans are being kept, if not in this folder.

☐ 13. Include in the folder any drawings or sketches or other data needed to get this job completed. If there is information that is not available yet, include a note below.

☐ 14. Put job on the scheduling board as soon as it can be scheduled with start date.

☐ 15. Plot the job out on the scheduling board all the way to completion date.

☐ 16. When at the site, take accurate field dimensions and fill in the **Required Tools Checklist** with as much data as possible so the installer will know what to bring.

☐ 17. Work out labor, materials, and any equipment needed and schedule as soon as possible.

☐ 18. **For field work:** travel, hotels, per diem payments, rental equipment, etc. must be worked out as early as possible to get the best pricing. Send all cost data to finance so it can be verified against the invoice if we are billed.

☐ 19. Put folder in "scheduled" bin until it is needed.

SHOP PRODUCTION MANAGER AND/ OR FIELD OPERATIONS MANAGER

☐ 20. Look over notes and drawings in the folder and determine what needs to be done.

☐ 21. Check with the production support manager to find out if any manpower and/ or materials have been set aside for this job. Use material from stock if possible.

☐ 22. Get your crew and materials and get the job done.

☐ 23. Maintain **SAFETY** standards while you work.

☐ 24. Inspect and verify correctness of all work when complete.

☐ 25. Get Sign-Off/Completion form signed by contractor/field superintendent/ owner if needed and put it in the folder.

☐ 26. When job is complete, send the folder to the quality control manager.

QUALITY CONTROL MANAGER

☐ 27. Inspect the job for quality. If any problems are found, get it corrected right away and then find out who is responsible they can be corrected and re-trained if needed.

☐ 28. When the project passes inspection, be sure to let all involved know and validate the personnel who did it.

☐ 29. Send the folder to the operations manager.

OPERATIONS MANAGER

☐ 30. Verify that all parts of job are complete in production so that the balance can be collected as soon as possible.

☐ 31. Send the folder to the finance manager.

FINANCE MANAGER

☐ 32. Take all of the paperwork from this folder and put it into the office folder. Follow the office folder routing form from this point on.

End of Routing Form. File this routing form in the folder with all other data.

CHAPTER EIGHT REFERENCES:

(1) Policy 22 January 1972 Issue II, PERSONNEL PROGRAMMING, written by L Ron Hubbard

Mr. Hubbard says:

"A program is defined as: A plan of procedure; a schedule or system under which action may be taken toward a desired goal. The keynote is a sequence of actions."

(2) Policy 21 September 1970RA, Revised and Reissued 13 March 2013, STUDY DEFINITIONS, written by L. Ron Hubbard.

Mr. Hubbard says:

"CHECKLIST: A list of actions or inspections to ready an activity or machinery or object for use or estimate the needful repairs or corrections."

(3) Policy 9 August 1979RA, Issue II, Revised 31 December 2000, SERVICE PRODUCT OFFICER, written by L. Ron Hubbard.

Mr. Hubbard says:

"In order for org lines to flow, routing forms (RFs) must be used. A routing form is a full step-by-step road map on which a particle travels."

(I want to make sure you understand the concept of the word *particle* as it is used above. It is any person or thing, such as, a piece of paper, object, machine, materials or tools. A particle could be anything that can travel on a path through the company.)

And there you have it. I realize that there is a fair amount work involved in coming up with these checklists. I promise you, once done and used, all your operations become streamlined and enable your company to operate efficiently and with minimal error. You can download these checklists as digital files at www.NutsandBoltsContracting. com/resources.

In addition to the checklists mentioned above, the website also offers a variety of tools and tips to help you and your company excel including a newsletter, blog, latest industry news, and more. Check it out at www.NutsandBoltsContracting.com. So now we come to the end of this book and my pledge to you. I am here to assist you as a troubleshooter, consultant, and trainer for you, your company, and its executives or employees.

In closing, I would like to thank you for purchasing and reading this book. I trust it will help you avoid the pitfalls, kinks, and agony that I went through and at the same time help you achieve your goals and dreams.

Sincerely,

Joel Anderson

DID YOU ENJOY READING THIS BOOK?

If you enjoyed reading this book and found the information of value, please consider leaving a positive review on Amazon so others in our industry can find it. If there was anything you felt should be changed or added please email us at Joel@NutsandBoltsContracting.com.

About Joel Anderson

J oel Anderson is a construction industry consultant who works with construction, contracting, and trade professionals showing them how to strengthen their businesses, practices, and performance, enabling stable expansion of their activities and bottom line.

With over forty-six years of experience, Joel knows the business from bottom to top, inside and out. From personal experience, he knows the problems that companies and their management confront on a daily basis. Joel is especially talented at identifying these problems and implementing solutions to help take company operations to never-before-thought-of levels of production and growth.

Joel has provided successful services, both managerial and technical, for some of the biggest contracting corporations in the world including: Hensel-Phelps, CH2MHill, Mero Structures, Metso Power and Mining, USDOT, USDOD, USCG, and USPS, as well as many smaller companies. In his words, "My greatest joy is helping people succeed in their endeavors, whether in business or in life, as these are symbiotic."

He has been a lead player on many high-profile projects including:

- **Electrician, chief mechanical officer, and trainmaster for Ringling Bros. & Barnum and Bailey Circus, where he was responsible for the circus trains that transported the circus on its routes through North and Central America.**

- **Installation of stainless-steel dream catcher in the roof of the national Indian Museum in Washington, DC.**

- **Restoration of the structural steel on the Pentagon after 9/11.**

- **Built and erected the shuttle hangar at the National Air and Space Museum Steven Udvar Hazy Center in Chantilly, VA, where the space shuttle Challenger is on display.**

- **Installed all the support structure and the glass wall American flag at the Baltimore Flag House Museum.**

Joel has received recognition as an Honored Member in Strathmore's Who's Who and America's Registry of Outstanding Professionals. He has been honored as an opinion leader and appointed as a Florida Small Business Representative and was awarded Business Man of the Year twice. He was also presented with the President's National Leadership Award by the National Business Advisory Council. Joel has also received the President's Lifetime Volunteer Service Award for his continuous involvement in community and civic activities.

TESTIMONIALS FROM CLIENTS

"*As a contractor under my organization, Mr. Anderson has performed work ranging from custom re-fabrication of original historical iron handrails to structural steel assemblies for many facilities on our campus. Mr. Anderson has consistently been trusted for the most demanding projects where quality, speed, and trade coordination are paramount. In fact, it was he who was trusted to install the massive cross on the top of our 365,000-square-foot cathedral while it was being filmed and watched by a countless number of our parishioners.*

What's more, Joel Anderson operates on a higher motivating principle than money, time, or accolades. I have noticed that he is driven by a determination to help people and to bring simplicity to seemingly complicated situations. Joel is a rare individual who has consistently demonstrated competence at every turn and he is the foundation of many successes of our organization."

Alec Parodi, Landlord, CofS
FSO, Inc.

"*Besides Joel's considerable mechanical engineering expertise and ability to solve some of our more taxing design and production flow problems on the manufacturing side, it is his organizational acumen that has made Joel's consultations and advice so dramatically valuable.*

He has helped us debug our entire business hierarchy, making suggestions that have proven critical to opening up demand for our product and sales. Joel has streamlined our staff, helping us find 'camouflaged holes' where we thought a function was being handled when it wasn't, and so has greatly increased our productivity while saving us money.

Joel has insight and skills unmatched by any other consultant we have ever used in the manufacturing and construction industries. I cannot recommend him enough. I just wish he would let us hire him permanently!"

Ralf W. Blackstone, MD, Founder
Statim Technologies, LLC

"I have worked with Joel Anderson on several large projects in the past few years. I've always been impressed with his 'can do' attitude. No problem is too big or too impossible to solve.

When given a task, he attacks it with enthusiasm and creativity. After giving him a project, I've never had to worry whether it would be done correctly or delivered on time—often under budget. And he is a real pleasure to work with, too!"

Gregg Winteregg, Consultant
MGE Management Experts, Inc.

"Having worked with Joel Anderson on several projects I can tell you that his knowledge of structure, foundations, and building materials is unsurpassed by anyone that I know. And having been in both residential and commercial real estate for nearly thirty years, working constantly with contractors of all types, I have to know who to trust when there are serious issues at hand. The most trustworthy and knowledgeable person I can call is Joel."

Pamela Ryan, Real Estate Broker/Owner
Ryan Realty, Inc.

JOEL ANDERSON AS A COMMUNITY LEADER

"I have known and worked with Joel Anderson since 2009 and have always found him to be competent, dependable, and passionate.

We are both very active in our community and so have had the opportunity to work together on numerous charitable events and activities. Each time Joel was a driving force behind solving any problem that arose and doing so with a positive never-say-never attitude that ensures that the job gets done.

Whenever I end up with Joel on my team I know that our project will run smoothly and have a successful outcome."

Diane Stein, President
CCHR Florida

"Joel was and is the driving force behind the construction and de-construction of structures for a charity function that occurs every year during the Christmas season.

Early on I had the pleasure of helping Joel build large electrical panels that provided power to that charity function. He graciously showed me what was needed and wanted so that I could help him effectively.

Additionally, I consider Joel to be a master at operating heavy equipment. He has always positioned the loads precisely where they were needed—sometimes within an inch or so. Joel always seems to come up with the most elegant and simple solution to any construction issue."

Terry Slade, IT professional

"I have worked with Joel Anderson for the past six years during the holiday season. He is fully responsible for creating and building the Annual Winter Wonderland (a village filled with holiday spirit for the whole community to enjoy) in Clearwater, Florida. This includes running countless volunteers who may or may not be

knowledgeable in building trades, demonstrating his ability to communicate and teach while also getting an enormous project done!

I have been impressed on many occasions at his ability to find the most expedient solution to the countless problems that always arise on a building project. He does this with great competence and affability, which is what makes it so pleasant to work with Joel.

His foresight and ability to manage from beginning to end along with his strong character is what makes him the person you want running the job!"

Kannon Feshbach, Operations Coordinator

JOEL ANDERSON AS A FRIEND AND COLLEAGUE

"I have known Joel Anderson for over twenty years. During that time, I have had the fortunate opportunity of knowing him as an individual, benefitting from his professional acumen in business and people; I watched him expand and grow as a successful construction industry leader and most importantly I have perceived him as a person who is the embodiment of everything he helps others to be. He is a master of a person in the fullest sense of the word. And that is what you want in a friend and confidant—trust, integrity, and the leadership quality of setting a great example to others. I have never seen Joel falter from that standard. Plus, he's a hell of a lot of fun to be around!"

Joe Yazbeck, Leadership Trainer, Master Speaker, Best-Selling Author, Company Founder, Prestige Leadership Advisors

"I met Joel fifteen years ago on a job site and I was amazed at his solution-oriented approach, his competence, and his execution of the work.

Not long after, I sought him out as my employer and apprenticed under him. I took a large pay cut to start in a new career under him, by choice, but I knew it would be worth it. We worked together for more than ten years and the knowledge I learned from him about business and life is priceless. I owe my success to him.

He is the best employer, teacher, and friend I have ever had. I often say that I have adopted him (unofficially, of course) as my father. We still work together on many projects and volunteer events in our community and are very close friends."

Steve Bibeau, Vice President of Construction

"I have known Joel Anderson for over ten years and clearly remember the incredible impression Joel left on me the first time we met at a hotel renovation contractor's meeting. Out of about twenty contractors in that room, he was the most organized and knowledgeable of all. During that meeting, I was wondering who he was and could not wait until the meeting was over to go over and meet him personally. He handled all the customer's originations with such great communication and incredible knowledge of his field that you could tell Joel was not the typical contractor.

I have been involved in several projects with Joel and his work is always top notch. Additionally, Joel has a gracious personality, which makes working with him a pleasure, and he always displays the utmost competence, earning great respect from all his peers."

Pedro Prado, President
The Painter Company

NOTES

NOTES

NOTES

NOTES

Made in the USA
Columbia, SC
19 September 2020